Praise for *A Book About the Book*

A Book About the Book is a wonderful read for all believers no matter where one is with their walk with God. I also recommend it for non-believers who are searching for a biblical understanding of who GOD is. The author explains the Bible in such a down-to-earth fashion that readers will glean new understandings of scripture, no matter how many times they have read the Bible in the past.

I found myself drawn to reading this book each morning, not wanting to put it down. The author not only explains the scriptures, but guides the reader with questions to help them engage with different aspects of scripture and the Law. The author then enlightens us on that section of the Bible. He covers major differences between God's Law and God's Grace, and has done an outstanding job covering scripture from the creation in Genesis to what the Bible tells us in the book of Revelation, as well as many parts of the Bible in between. If you have been overwhelmed reading your Bible in the past, or have put your Bible down declaring to never pick it up again, you need to read this book. It will make understandable in a fresh way God's Word and what it means for you. My hope is that the author will continue to research and write more on other passages of scripture, as this book is about the unending story of how God's love and grace are available for all who will believe on His name.

—Terry Koglin

A Book About the Book is exactly what we needed to enhance our ability to understand and eternally benefit from God's word.

Reading this book has inspired us to go back into the Bible and discover God's word with a sense of confidence. The Bible is an amazing epic story of salvation brought to life with the author's guidance and his gift for simplifying the intricacies for us.

We have used the book to help guide our studies and have found it to aid in generating much discussion on topics such as grace, being born again, sin, forgiveness and resurrection.

The book clearly reduces the "intimidation factor" of interpreting the Bible. Like a well prepared message from our Pastor, Don's ability to retell or clarify scripture has made us want to dig deeper.

We do admit that we found there to be a great deal of information for one to comprehend in one's first read. We are intrigued by a new and exciting way to study the Bible revealed in *A Book About the Book*.

Some of our most in-depth discussion followed our reading of Chapter 15. We both feel strongly that the Bible is a book of action and we found this chapter, in particular, to be very personal and motivational for us. Simply believe in the one He sent and eternity is available to everyone. That's why Ephesians 2:8-9 is our favorite verse.

Don, it's clear your understanding of God's word is a gift from which we will surely benefit. Your work will help us be more prepared (through a greater understanding) while spreading the good news of salvation through Jesus Christ, at home and during our return mission trips in Honduras.

Thank-you.

—Gary & Kendra Ondrus

A Book About
THE BOOK

Comments or
questions call
me at

517 2635899

A Book About THE BOOK

Don Burack

A Book About the Book

dlburack@comcast.net

Published by Tate Publishing & Enterprises, LLC
127 E. Trade Center Terrace | Mustang, Oklahoma 73064 USA
1.888.361.9473 | www.tatepublishing.com

Tate Publishing is committed to excellence in the publishing industry. The company reflects the philosophy established by the founders, based on Psalm 68:11,
"The Lord gave the word and great was the company of those who published it."

Cover design by Samson Lim
Interior design by Richell Balansag

Published in the United States of America

ISBN: 978-1-68254-949-0
Religion / Christianity / General
15.12.09

Tate Publishing's Statement of Beliefs

Tate Publishing believes in the reality of one true God, eternal and infinite, existing as three persons—Father, Son, and Holy Spirit.

Man was made in the image of God. When the first man succumbed to the temptation of Satan and chose to disobey God, he brought sin and its curse upon the human race. Since the penalty of sin is death, as long as man lives in sin, he is dead spiritually and is facing physical death and eternal punishment in hell. This fall from grace put man in the position of needing forgiveness in order that his fellowship with God might be restored.

Because God had established that only the shedding of blood provides remission of sin, He sent His son, Jesus Christ, into the world to take man's sin upon Himself. Jesus was begotten by the Holy Spirit, born of the virgin Mary, and is true God and true man, the only sinless man who ever lived. As the lamb of God, He took man's sin upon Himself as He died on the cross, thus satisfying God's holy demands for all mankind.

He was buried, and was resurrected on the third day following His crucifixion. After appearing to various people during a period of forty days, He ascended into heaven and is the only mediator between God and man. All who personally receive Him, through faith, are declared righteous on the basis of His shed blood and not of their works of righteousness.

When a person confesses the fact that he is a sinner and acknowledges Jesus Christ as his Lord and Savior, his spirit is reborn. He becomes a new creation, a member of the true Church, indwelt by the Holy Spirit. This salvation is not the result of any human effort, but is the free gift of God's grace in Jesus Christ. Jesus Christ will physically return to the earth one day as King of Kings and Lord of Lords.

Jesus destroyed all the works of Satan, who as god of this world, is allowed to continue, for now, to blind the eyes of those who do not believe. Satan leads a host of fallen beings who are his aids in warring against believers. Believers must be aware of the reality of spiritual warfare and know that victory is theirs through the application of scriptural truth and the presence and power of the indwelling Spirit of Christ.

God sent His Holy Spirit with gifts to the Church to empower believers for witnessing of Jesus, as well as to be comforter and teacher, until Jesus comes again. The Holy Spirit convicts the world of sin, righteousness, and judgment. The Holy Spirit witnesses not unto Himself, but to the risen Christ. He regenerates, seals, anoints and sets apart the believer to a holy life.

Christ ordained the observance of water baptism and the Lord's supper until He returns.

The Bible was written by men who wrote under the direct control, inspiration, and anointing of God. The Bible does not contain the Word of God, it is the Word of God—the infallible, inerrant, only written revelation which God has given to man. It increases man's faith, as well as instructs and corrects him that he might become holy, separated from the world and unto God. The main theme of the Bible is God's plan of salvation in Jesus Christ. Everything in the life of every human being is directly or indirectly affected by his attitude about the Bible—whether or not he accepts it as the inspired Word of God. It is the supreme and final authority in all matters about which it speaks.

Acknowledgments

Many thanks to my wife, Linda, for her encouragement and dedicated spirit. Without her help and encouragement, this book could not have been written.

Contents

Foreword

While reading Don's book, *A Book About the Book*, I was glad to see that he used many references from the Bible to explain his take on various subjects, and not just his opinion. Don's writing on prayer was very well done. It was especially good to read all the supporting verses that he used in his study. The way Don divided the sections of prayer under law and prayer under grace was very interesting and thought provoking. He also divided the teaching under law and Paul's teaching under grace, which marks the time before and after Christ's death. It made a lot of sense the way he developed these two concepts. I was fascinated by Don's handling of the timelines of God's plan for mankind. The process by which he put together three timelines really made me think. If Don wrote this book to stimulate in us the urge to study the Bible, he certainly has accomplished his goal. It is evident that he has used many hours of prayer and Bible study in completing this writing. Thank you, Don, for sharing with us your thoughts, insights and biblical knowledge.

Blessings to you,

—Paul Palpant
Elementary Principal-Retired
Lenawee Christian School

Preface

The Bible is, for the most part, a very hard book to comprehend. It is easier to understand if you are able to keep things in perspective. Leave things where they are. If they are the Jews under the law of Moses and the covenants of God, keep them there. Do not try to bring them into the church age because they just do not fit. And do not try to put the church age of grace under the law—it does not fit. You can't put a one-inch square peg into a one-inch round hole. It just won't fit even though they are the same size. We know this, so we don't even try. Yet we try to mix law and grace then wonder why some scriptures do not make sense. They just don't fit, yet we keep trying. Keep these separate, and all of a sudden the whole Bible comes together as you have never seen before.

God created man for fellowship, yet in such a way that man could choose to fellowship with him or not. In God's foreknowledge, he knew that man would sin, so in the determinant counsel of God, they set forth a plan of redemption to bring man back into fellowship. God loves all people, but not all people love God.

After Adam sinned, the whole human race that followed Adam, were under the curse of sin. God called Abraham from among this fallen race of people to call out a people for himself that became known as the nation of Israel. At this time, God had planned for Israel to become a light unto the Gentiles. If they would just do as God commanded them, they would be blessed.

When God brought them up out of Egypt to the gateway to the Promised Land, he told them to go in and possess the land and that he would drive the inhabitants out with hornets. But they did not trust God, so they sent in spies, then decided not to enter for fear of the giant men. God then sent them into the wilderness for forty years. If they would have just trusted God, they could have had it all. Had they done what God wanted them to do, no one would have been killed. The Jews have been fighting wars ever since.

God sent his son to fulfill the law and the prophets—to save his people, Israel. Again they rejected God's offer. They could have had the kingdom that had been promised to them. The King, Jesus, was right there in their midst, but they rejected and crucified him.

God doesn't keep changing his mind. He knew in his foreknowledge that his offers would be rejected, yet he gave them the opportunity. Because of their disobedience, they would have to suffer the consequences of their decisions. Since the people of Israel would not be going out to the Gentiles, God called Paul to be the apostle to the Gentiles.

Listed below are four dispensations to keep in mind as you study your Bible. Keep them separate. They each have a beginning and an ending; do not mix them, keep them in their rightful place.

1. The dispensation of all people (Genesis 1 through 10)
2. The dispensation of the Jew's under law (Genesis 11 through Acts 8)
3. The dispensation of the church age under grace (Paul's epistles)
4. The dispensation of the kingdom (The return of the Jews in the book of Revelation)

The Bible consists of the Old and New Testaments. After the last book of the Old Testament was written, there is a period of four hundred years that are known as the silent years. In Christ's time here on earth, all of his biblical knowledge and his scriptural references were from the Old Testament. The New Testament was not written until between 37 to 96 AD.

The Bible is a history book that is full of facts—a book of books, sixty-six in all. It is the inspired written word of God. The men that wrote these books were inspired by the Holy Spirit.

> All scripture is given by inspiration of God, and is profitable for doctrine, for reproof, for correction, for instruction in righteousness: That

> the man of God may be perfect, thoroughly furnished unto all good works. (2 Tim. 3:16–17)

This brings us to an understanding that the Bible is God's words to us, mankind. However, unless you come to a saving knowledge of Jesus Christ, you will not be able to understand the spiritual aspects of the Bible.

> But God hath chosen the foolish things of the world to confound the wise; and God hath chosen the weak things of the world to confound the things which are mighty; and base things of the world, and things which are despised, hath God chosen, yea, and things which are not, to bring to naught things that are; That no flesh should glory in his presence. (1 Cor. 1:27–29)

> But the natural man receiveth not the things of the Spirit of God: for they are foolishness unto him: neither can he know them, because they are spiritually discerned. (1 Cor. 2:14)

In other words, unless you are a born again child of God—born of the spirit—you cannot comprehend spiritual things. You can understand earthly or worldly things, like the historical facts of the Bible, but you cannot understand the spiritual.

The Bible is also a road map. Getting us from point A to point B. Point A being where we are now, lost and confused without God in our lives. Point B being the position that God intends for us to be in, in the future. Do you want to go to heaven? The Bible tells us how to get there. A road map to heaven. Can it get any better? As you read, you will be following the road map.

Let's say for example that you were looking for a friend that lives in Billings, Montana, and you have the street address. But all that you know is that it is somewhere out west, you have no idea how to get there. So what do you do? You go to your computer, pull up MapQuest, type in the address, and you get a printout of a suggested route that will get you right to the driveway. This is what the Bible does for us.

The Bible leads us to an acknowledgement of who Christ is and what he has done for us. As we read the Bible, we will come to the understanding of who God is, how he relates to mankind, and how mankind has responded to him. More often than not, man has either responded in a negative way or not at all. Throughout the Bible the Israelites, God's favored nation, have failed by not following God's leading.

In this book, the author will endeavor to teach you the basics of God's written word. How to keep things in context and not to blenderize scriptures by mixing them together. We get things all mixed up and then wonder why we can't understand them. The following are a couple of examples. In Matthew 21:18–20 Jesus curses the fig tree for not bearing fruit, and it quickly dries up and dies. The disciples are amazed by this. How can Jesus do this?

> Jesus answered and said unto them, verily I say unto you, if ye have faith, and doubt not, ye shall not only do this which is done to the fig

> tree, but also if ye shall say unto this mountain, Be thou removed, and be thou cast into the sea; it shall be done. And all things, whatsoever ye shall ask in prayer, believing, ye shall receive. (Matt. 21:21–22)

Was Jesus talking to you? No. Then who was he talking to? He was talking to the disciples. So why can't I do these miracles or get what I want when I pray? Because I am not one of the disciples; I am a member of the body of Christ, the true church that the disciples knew nothing about.

> And when he had called unto him his twelve disciples, he gave them power against unclean spirits, to cast them out, and to heal all manner of sickness and all manner of disease. (Matt. 10:1)

Read Acts 3:1–11 to get the flow of this last example.

> Then Peter said, silver and gold have I none, but such as I have give I thee; In the name of Jesus Christ of Nazareth rise up and walk. (Acts 3:6)

Unless God has given you power as he did the Twelve, I wouldn't try this unless you want to be embarrassed or humiliated. Remember to keep things in perspective, in their proper place. Jesus gave his disciples power to accomplish miracles and to receive what they asked for. Not you and I—let that sink in.

Things to think about: When we die, does the spirit or soul have the ability to think or remember? The memory is a function of the brain. The brain is a part of the body; when the body dies, so does the brain. Is there an end to space? If you were to reach the end of space, what would be on the other side? How can you explain eternity? Do we spend eternity in the third heaven where God is? Will this earth ever come to an end? What will happen to earth when the sun burns out? Will the sun burn out? Where did God live while he created heaven and earth? If Genesis 1:3–5 was the first day, what day was Genesis 1:1? John 3:13 states that no man has ascended to heaven; what happened to Enoch and Elijah? Why did God choose Mary to be the mother of Jesus? In Matthew 1 the genealogy of Jesus is different from the one in Luke 3. Why? You will find the answers to some of these thought-provoking questions as you continue reading.

Introduction

This book takes the reader on a quick trip through time from Adam to the present, answering many questions such as the following: Where did the light come from on day one since the sun, moon, and stars were not created until the fourth day? Were Adam and Eve created at the same time? God is said to be omnipresent, meaning that he is everywhere at all times. Is he in the heart of a nonbeliever? Is God in hell? Is Satan in hell? Has he ever been in hell? Will he ever be in hell? Do you know the difference between the church in the book of Acts and the churches that Paul started?

Jesus said that he would lay down his life for many. Paul said that Jesus died for all. Why the difference? Jesus is the son of God, but is he the son of the heavenly Father? Before Jesus died on the cross, he commanded his disciples not to go to the Gentiles but to go only to the lost sheep of Israel. After the cross, he commanded them to go out into the whole world and preach the gospel. Why the difference? In Genesis 13, God told Abram that his seed would be as many as the dust of the earth. In chapter 15, God told Abram that his seed would be as many as the stars in the sky. Why? As you read the Bible, don't be afraid to ask questions. When you see something that doesn't line up, don't just drop it; pursue it, until you get an answer. Usually the Holy Spirit will show you as you read the scriptures. Often it is just common sense.

Ask yourself why this verse is in the Bible and how does it compare with other scriptures. Take notes as you read. Ask God to give you understanding as you study, and he will. One of the purposes of this book is to spur your interest in reading your Bible. If that be true for you, then my goal has been accomplished.

SECTION I

1

A Panoramic View of the Bible

The Bible is a book of books. There are thirty-nine books in the Old Testament and twenty-seven books in the New Testament. There is a division between book thirty-nine and forty. The first thirty-nine books are about how God dealt with the Israelites from Abraham, Moses, and the prophets under the law. The twenty-seven books of the New Testament introduces us to Jesus Christ, the Messiah. Thirty-nine books before the Messiah and twenty-seven books after the Messiah. Sixty-six books in all.

The book of Isaiah has sixty-six chapters, thirty-nine chapters before the captivity by the Assyrians and twenty-seven chapters after the captivity. The book of Isaiah is like a Bible inside the Bible.

Something else of interest: Psalms 118 is approximately the center of the Bible. Chapter 117 is the shortest chapter in the Bible, having only two verses. Chapter 119 is the longest, having 176 verses.

The sixty-six books of the Bible were written by forty different writers over a period of 1,600 years without contradicting each other. Now that is amazing in light of what Christianity is like today. No matter what one Christian group believes, there is another group that will disagree.

The first five books of the Bible were written by Moses. These five books are called the Pentateuch. Genesis is the book of beginnings and the introduction of sin and disobedience. Exodus is a book of redemption. Leviticus is a book of obedience, worship, and communion. Numbers is a book of the wandering Jewish nation looking for their promised inheritance. Deuteronomy is a book about their past and future in the Promised Land. The rest of the Old Testament books are called historical books, with the possible exception of Job, a more philosophical book. This, of course, includes the major and minor prophets.

Genesis begins with the creation of all things, including mankind. Adam and Eve. Just the first two chapters leave me with a lot of questions. On the first day God created light; where did the light come from that separated day from night? He didn't create the sun, moon, and stars until the fourth day. Why didn't God create Adam and Eve at the same time? Or did he?

As you read the Bible I am sure that you also will have a lot of questions. When I look through the Bible to get these answers, I usually end up with more questions than answers. And this is what keeps me studying the scriptures.

Sin and its consequences are revealed in chapter 3. The book of Genesis covers the first 2,300 years, and they go by quickly. Chapter 6 is about Noah and the flood; 1,650 have gone by already. Oh, my, how time flies.

Abram, later known as Abraham, is introduced in chapter 11. It is through his seed, or descendents that the nation of Israel will be formed. God made a covenant with Abraham that God would build a nation beginning with Abraham's seed. A covenant is a promise from God that he cannot break. There are eight covenants in the Bible.

Abraham, Isaac, and Jacob are known throughout the Bible as the fathers of the Israelites. Jacob was the grandson of Abraham. God changed Jacob's name to Israel. Jacob had twelve sons. These twelve sons later became known as the twelve tribes of Israel.

Then comes Joseph and the 400 years in Egypt in captivity. Then Moses and the burning bush, which leads to the exodus from Egypt. During their forty years in the wilderness, God gave Moses the Ten Commandments. The law is established. What started as ten laws became 613 by the time of Christ's ministry.

Moses governed the people along with Aaron. The people were not satisfied with this, so God appointed judges and then kings. Through the leadership of Joshua, the people entered the Promised Land, now known as Israel. We are skipping a lot of history here just covering the highlights.

The nation of Israel repeatedly fell short of God's expectations, and God continually gave them opportunity to repent. God set up priests for their spiritual guidance. All priests would be a go-between for the people and God.

Now we are at the birth of Jesus. Something that you may not understand at this point is that Jesus' ministry was to the Jews only. I'll explain this in a later chapter. Every promise to the Israelites was earthly. The kingdom of heaven that the Israelites were expecting is Christ's earthly kingdom that will last one thousand years.

The Jews under the law were never promised anything that was heavenly. They were looking for the Messiah to set up his kingdom in Jerusalem. On Palm Sunday, when Jesus rode into the city of Jerusalem, they thought that he would throw out the Romans and set up the promised kingdom. He did not, and they rejected him as their Messiah.

This brings us to Paul in the book of Acts. So far, since Abraham, the Bible deals only with the Jewish nation. It is all about the Jews. But now things are about to change. We are entering into the dispensation of grace.

Paul wrote thirteen books of the New Testament, plus I give him credit for the book of Hebrews. Saul, later to be known as Paul, was on the road to Damascus when Jesus appeared to him. A mystery is revealed to Paul. In scripture, a mystery is something that God has kept secret. Jesus directs Paul to go to the Gentiles and preach to them this new gospel.

The book of Revelation is the culmination of all things. Revelation 21 and 22 talk about a new heaven and a new earth, where we will spend eternity with God if we are his children.

As we study the Bible, it is easier to understand if we can keep things in perspective as to who, what, when, where, and why and then ask yourself, how does this apply to me? Keep things in context.

This is where spiritual discernment comes into play. If you do not understand spiritual things, you will have a tendency to be thinking historically. We that are born again spiritually are in the world but are not of the world. If you are not spiritually discerned, you may not understand the following.

When you read something from Matthew you will find Jesus dealing with the Jews. When you read from Romans, you find Paul dealing with the true church, the body of Christ, known as Christians. Two completely different dispensations. A dispensation is a period of time that God sets aside for his purposes.

Jesus dealt with the Jews under the law. Paul dealt with Christians under grace. You cannot mix the two; it is like trying to mix oil and water. You can mix them up, but the oil will soon come to the top. We often blenderize scriptures and then wonder why we cannot understand what we just read. It just doesn't make sense to us.

When we read the Bible we see these words often: *if, and, but, therefore, until*. Don't miss the meaning of these words as you read. The word *if* is a word of choice. If you keep my commandments, I will bless you. Right away you should see that there is an opposite choice. If you do not keep my commandments, I will curse you.

The word *and* is a word of continuation or in addition to. I find it interesting that in my King James Bible, in Genesis 1 the first word in every verse is *and* except two verses: the first and the twenty-seventh. The word *and* is used ninety-one times in this first chapter.

When you see the word *but* we find that it denotes an opposing view or flipside. *If* and *but* are at times interchangeable, often giving a choice and its consequences.

When you see the word *therefore*, back up and read the previous verses to find out what it is there for. And the word *until* is a time word.

Don't miss these small, seemingly unimportant words; they often set the stage for what you are about to read. Also, remember to ask yourself who is writing and to whom is it being written. When, where, and why was it written. You will be amazed at your understanding when you apply this reasoning. Then ask yourself, how does this apply to me?

Now a quote from Corrie Ten Boom. "If you look at the world, you will be distressed. If you look within you will be depressed. But if you look to Christ, you will be at rest."

Here is the Bible in a nutshell as told by Dr. James Kennedy:

> Genesis 1 and 2—generation
> Genesis 3—degeneration
> The rest of the Bible—regeneration

A question for you to think about. What do the first two chapters of the Bible and the last two chapters of the Bible have in common? Read them and think about this question. You will find the answer in a later chapter.

Here is an exercise to get you thinking. Connect all of the dots with four straight lines. Do not lift your pencil or retrace any lines.

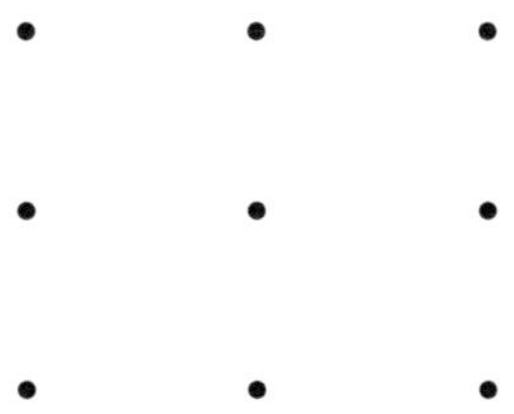

At first this may seem impossible, but it can be done. Don't give up right away. Keep trying; there is a very important message here. The answer will be found in chapter 2.

2

The Creation Story

Chronologically, John 1:1 comes before Genesis 1:1.

> In the beginning was the Word, and the Word was with God, and the Word was God. (John 1:1)

> In the beginning God created the heaven and the earth. (Gen. 1:1)

God created the heaven and the earth. The word *the* is singular, yet we know that there are three heavens because God's throne is in the third heaven. So here we are talking about the first heaven. This is our sky, which may include our solar system and possibly our galaxy. The second heaven would be the rest of the universe. The first heaven is now Satan's domain; he is the prince and the power of the air.

As we look at the six days of creation in the first two chapters of Genesis, we need to have an open mind. There are many things written in the Bible that we are not able to comprehend because God has not revealed all things to us. Some things are to be taken by faith—God said it, believe it even if you can't understand what you read.

Sometimes science runs counter to the Bible. At times proving but never disproving. Usually their theories are just that, theories and conjecture, not fact. As you read the Bible you will have a lot of questions. Write them down, and as you read further, you will find that the Bible will answer most of your questions. Keep an open mind and think outside of the box. Oh, by the way, that is the answer to the dot exercise: think outside of the box.

In order to solve this problem, you have to go outside of the imaginary box. I say imaginary because you boxed the dots in when there is no box. This is how our mind works. We put limits or restrictions on our thinking. Open up a little and allow for other possibilities. Now try the dots again, and if you still can't do it, you will find the answer at the end of this chapter.

In many scriptures there is room for your own understanding. Different ways to understand or interpret what that scripture means to you. If you are wrong, you will receive more light on the subject as you read some other scriptures. The Holy Spirit will not leave you in the dark.

I am not going to attempt to try to explain every verse in the Bible. That is what the Holy Spirit of God will do as you study. My attempt will be to bring certain scriptures to light to show you what the Bible has to say about many different subjects.

Not only do scientists have theories, but biblical scholars have theories also. The most renowned theory is the gap theory. This being that there could be millions or billions of years between verse 1 and verse 2 of Genesis 1.

"In the beginning." In the beginning of what? The Bible was written for mankind. It would therefore be understood that "in the beginning" would mean in the beginning of mankind. This could mean that God made heaven and earth billions of years ago, and the dinosaurs roamed and caveman lived a long time before God started to get the earth ready for Adam and Eve.

Some theologians believe that Lucifer was cast out of heaven after his encounter with God, when he tried to usurp God's throne, and here is where verse 2 comes into play. The earth was made billions of years ago, and it was just like the earth in Adam's day. Because everything that God made was good, why make a world that had no shape or form, they reason. Because of Satan's fall from heaven, the earth became formless and void, and then God regenerated the earth to get it ready for mankind. This begins in verse 3.

God said, "Let us make man in our image." Here in is the first revealing that God is a triune God. He said "our" image—our meaning more than one. God made man more like himself than he made the caveman. Adam was created with a soul and a spirit, as well as a body. The caveman was just a body—an animal. He had no God consciousness.

According to this theory there are only three days of created acts. The other three are regeneration of the existing earth before the first great flood that covered the whole earth.

The sun, moon, and stars were created in verse 1. On day 1, God let the light appear; he didn't create it now. On day 2, he separated the waters, and some of the water formed clouds that shrouded the whole earth. On day 3, the grass and trees grew from the seeds that were in the earth. On day 4, the sun, moon, and stars were already here, and God allowed the clouds to come together, and the heavenly lights became visible. On day 5, God created the fish and fowl. On day 6, God created animals and man. Genesis 2:4 says:

> These are the generations of the heavens and of the earth when they were created, in the day that the Lord God made the earth and the heavens.

Generations are usually considered to be more than one day. It also says "in the day." So a day here is an unspecified period of time. So what are we supposed to believe? I believe that God created the heavens, the earth, and everything that was needed for mankind. And He did it in six days and stopped working and rested from His work on the seventh day. This is what the Bible teaches, and I believe this even though I don't understand it all.

Now is it possible that there were billions of years between verse 1 and 2? Yes. Is it possible that cavemen existed before Adam? Yes. Is it possible that oil, gas, and coal formed over billions of years? Yes. With God, all things are possible. Does it make any difference to you how God does what He does? It should be sufficient to accept the light that God gives us and to be thankful for that light.

There may be some validity in what these theorists say because I have trouble trying to understand where the light came from on day 1. There was enough light to separate day from night. The evening and the morning were the first day. This is what the sun, moon, and stars do, but they were not created until the forth day! Or were they?

> So God created man in his own image, in the image of God created he him; male and female created he them. (Gen. 1:27)

> Male and female created He them; and blessed them, and called their name Adam in the day when they were created. (Gen. 5:2)

God created man and woman at one time, in one body, and called their name Adam.

Adam is a word from Hebrew, *adham*, meaning "man" or *adhamak* meaning "man from earth." Adam, the male, named the female Eve in Genesis 3:20. Up until then she was referred to as woman or Adam's wife. The Bible relates to us that God created man and woman, and He did it on the sixth day, and their name was Adam.

Some theologians or theorist say that God created man and woman at the same time, and they had a struggle for power or leadership, and the woman left, possibly later becoming Cain's wife. And then God created another woman from Adam's rib so that Adam would be in control. To me, this sounds like God made a mistake the first time and had to do it again. But God does not make mistakes.

God named two trees in the Garden of Eden. Why only two trees? One was called the tree of the knowledge of good and evil and the other was the tree of life. This is by design to give man a choice.

Adam chose to eat of the fruit from the tree of knowledge of good and evil. And God expelled him from the garden of eden. Why?

> And the Lord God said. Behold, the man is become as one of us, to know good and evil; and now, lest he put forth his hand, and take also of the tree of life, and eat, and live for ever. (Gen. 3:22)

Had Adam eaten from the tree of life after his sin, he would have lived forever in his sin, so God kept Adam from doing so by expelling him from the garden.

Now think for a minute, what would have happened had Adam eaten from the tree of life and not the forbidden tree? I think you would come to the same conclusion that I have. That is, God would have to get rid of the tree of the knowledge of good and evil so that Adam would not eat from it and live forever in sin.

Did the serpent lie to Eve? Yes and no.

> Now the serpent was more subtil than any beast of the field which the Lord God had made. And he said unto the woman , Yea, hath God said, Ye shall not eat of every tree in the garden? And the woman said unto the serpent, We may eat of the fruit of the trees of the garden: But the fruit of the tree which is in the midst of the garden, God hath said, Ye shall not eat of it, neither shall ye touch it lest ye die. (Gen. 3:1–3)

The woman, Eve, added to God's word when she said "neither shall ye touch it." I think at this point Satan knew that he had her on the ropes and he didn't have to lie to her.

> And the serpent said unto the woman, ye shall not surely die; For God doth know that in the day ye eat thereof, then your eyes shall be opened, and ye shall be as gods, knowing good and evil. (Gen. 3:4–5)

The serpent told Eve that she would not die, and she didn't. He said that she would be as a god, knowing good and evil. Did she? Yes. So did the serpent lie to her? No and yes. When God said that they would die, he was talking about spiritual death, and the serpent was talking about physical death. And that is how he deceived Eve.

Now Eve was deceived by the serpent, Satan, but Adam ate of the fruit by choice. Why would Adam chose to disobey God? Did he want to keep harmony with his wife? Did he trust in the woman because God had given her to him? I don't know. But according to verse 12, Adam makes it sound that way.

> And the man said, The woman whom thou gavest to be with me, she gave me of the tree, and I did eat. (Gen. 3:12)

Adam's sin was disobedience to God. This is known in the Bible as the fall of Adam. And because of his sin, all of his seed, the whole of mankind, are by nature born in sin. So we find that the whole human race is sinful.

Adam's fall from God's grace presents a problem for Adam and all of mankind, as well as a problem for God. God created man for fellowship. He walked with Adam in the garden. God wanted to be with Adam, but sin separated them.

Herein is the dilemma, Adam cannot come to God, and God will not come to Adam because of sin. So it is God's move. He can do something about the situation, Adam cannot. God implements the sacrifice of animals, that the blood of the animal will be shed to hide or cover the sins of mankind. God does this in Genesis 3:21.

> Unto Adam also and to his wife did the Lord God make coats of skins, and clothed them.

This sacrifice of the animal looks forward to the day that God will sacrifice his Son on the cross to pay for mankind's sin debt.

Cain and Abel

Cain is the eldest son of Adam; Abel was his younger brother. God called for them to bring a blood sacrifice before the Lord. Abel did well, but Cain did not. Abel was found to be righteous in his offering. Cain's offering was not accepted of God, and Cain became wroth with God, and God said that sin lieth at your door. But Cain did not repent.

Cain killed his brother, Abel. Some may say that he did not know that by hitting his brother with a rock or club that it would kill his brother. Death for humans was unknown at this time. In any case it happened, and Cain was exiled to wander the earth. He married and had children.

Obvious question, who did Cain marry? We do not know how many years have gone by nor how old Cain would have been. There is no explanation found in the Bible as far as I can see, so I assume that he would have married another descendant of Adam—his sister.

Eve then gave birth to Seth. He was to replace Abel. Abel was righteous, Cain was not. The heads of two different civilizations. Actually, that would be Seth, not Abel, because Seth replaced Abel. The genealogy of Christ in Luke 3:23–38 follows the line of Seth, not Cain.

As you read the Bible look for places where the firstborn is worldly and the younger sibling is heavenly or righteous. Here are some examples.

Cain	worldly
Abel	righteous
Adam	worldly
Christ	righteous
Esau	worldly
Jacob	righteous

Now we will cover the flood of Noah's days.

We are only in chapter 6, and 1,500 years have gone by already. Noah, in the linage of Seth, was found of God to be righteous, and he was apparently the only one out of what must have been millions of people.

God gave Noah instructions to build an ark (a type of Christ) to be saved from the worldwide flood that was to come. Out of all the inhabitance of the earth, there were only eight souls saved from or through the flood. Noah preached of the coming flood for over one hundred years as he built the ark, yet nobody believed his message. Does this sound like today? Many people hear the gospel being preached, yet few respond to his call.

Now here is where God's grace is so plainly shown, but most people miss this. After all of the animals and Noah and his family were in the ark, Noah left the door open for seven days. And the Lord shut him in. Had Noah shut the door himself, he would have wondered for the rest of his life, *If I would have left the door open for just one more day, maybe I could have saved some.* But God shut the door so that Noah would be free from that burden. God opens and closes doors for us also, but sometimes we don't recognize that he does.

All that we have covered so far is for our learning and understanding as to how things began. Next we will come to Abram and how the Jewish nation came to be. When we get to Abram, later to be known as Abraham, two thousand years have passed, and we are only in chapter 11. It will take another two thousand years and the rest of the book of Genesis and all of the Old Testament to get us to the birth of Christ.

Before we get to the next chapter on Abram, I want to cover something that is hard to explain or to understand. And that is Genesis 6:1–4. The sons of God took the daughters of men, married them, and had children. The sons of God are often thought of as being the angels that lost their first estate in Jude 1:6, but this cannot be because they are chained up.

> And the angels which kept not their first estate; but left their own habitation, He hath reserved in everlasting chains under darkness unto the judgment of the great day.

I believe that the sons of God are here referring to the linage of Seth, and the daughters of men are of the linage of Cain. Because of interbreeding between these two cultures, the whole human race became corrupt.

> And God saw that the wickedness of man was great in the earth and that every imagination of the thoughts of his heart was only evil continually. (Gen 6:5)

And now the answer to the dot exercise.

I am trying to get you to think outside of the box of your mind, broaden your horizons. Don't just assume something that your church teaches or your preacher preaches is completely true or all inclusive; read your Bible and let the Holy Spirit guide you.

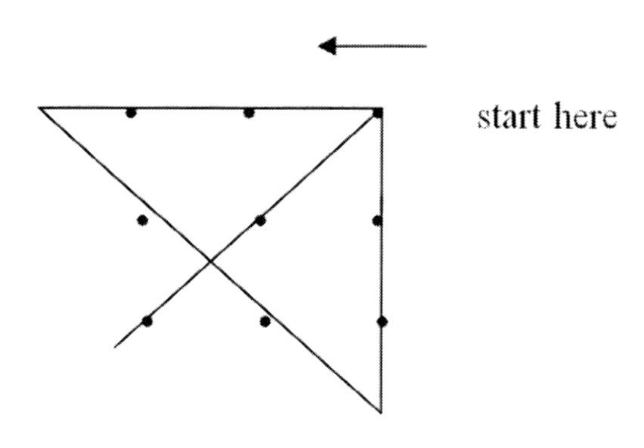

3

The Nation of Israel

Abram was called of God to set himself and his wife, Sarai, apart from his kinsmen. After the flood, now 500 years later, the whole world had again returned to idolatry and turned away from God. God chose Abram to be the father of the nation of Israel.

> Now the Lord had said unto Abram, Get thee out of thy country, and from thy kindred, and from thy father's house unto a land that I will shew thee, And I will make of thee a great nation, and I will Bless thee, and make thy name great; and thou shall be a blessing; And I will bless them that bless thee, and curse him that curseth thee: and in thee shall all families of the earth be blessed. (Gen. 12:1–3)

Now contrast this with Genesis 17:4–5:

> As for me, behold my covenant is with thee, and thou shalt be a father of many nations, Neither shall thy name anymore be called Abram, but

> thy name shall be Abraham; for a father of many nations have I made thee.

What happened? He went from the father of a great nation to the father of many nations. You can read this for yourself, and I hope that you do, but I will give you a synopsis of what happened.

God promised a son to Abram and Sarai when Abram was eighty years old and Sarai was seventy. Sarai, now seventy-six years old, offered her Egyptian housekeeper, Hagar, to Abram so that he could father a son with her. Hagar gave birth to Ishmael. Fourteen years later, when Sarai became pregnant herself, she ran Hagar and Ishmael off because she did not want this worldly woman and her son to be an influence on her son of promise. Did you notice? Ishmael, the eldest son—worldly—and Isaac the younger—righteous, the son of promise.

Ishmael later married and had twelve sons that became the Arabic nations. Abraham's grandson Jacob later married and had twelve sons that became the twelve tribes of Israel. Abraham became the father of a great nation, Israel, and the father of many nations because of the twelve sons of Ishmael.

Both Israelites and the Arab nations have Abraham as their father. But the promise or covenant that God had made with Abram was to his seed through the promised son Isaac.

You will notice that throughout the Bible when the Israelites refer to their fathers, it is always Abraham,

Isaac, and Jacob. They always refer to that lineage. Arabic nations refer to their father Abraham only. The covenant or promise that God made with Abraham continues with Jacob. That his seed will become the great nation of Israel.

Another point of interest to me is Sarai; her name became Sarah after the birth of Isaac. Sarai was Abram's wife, but she was also his half-sister. As you read these scriptures, you may be amazed, as I am, at how young and apparently beautiful-looking she must have been.

> And it came to pass when he was come near to enter into Egypt, that he said unto Sarai his wife, Behold now, I know that thou art a fair woman to look upon: Therefore it shall come to pass, when the Egyptians shall see thee, that they shall say, this is his wife: and they will kill me, but they will save thee alive. Say, I pray thee, thou art my sister that it may be well with me for thy sake; and my soul shall live because of thee. (Gen. 12:11–13)

The Egyptians beheld the woman that she was very fair, and they took her to the house of Pharaoh. Sarai would be sixty-five years old now as she was ten years younger than Abram.

> And Abraham said of Sarah his wife, She is my sister: and Abimelech, king of Gerar sent, and took Sarah. (Gen. 20:2)

At this point in time, Sarah would be at least ninety years old and apparently looked pretty good to Abimelech. Again, he used his wife to save his skin.

Now skip to Genesis 26:7. "And the men of the place asked him of his wife; and he said she is my sister; for he feared to say, She is my wife, lest said he, the men of the place should kill me for Rebekah; because she was fair to look upon." This is Abraham's son, Isaac. Like father like son, they say.

Circumcision

Circumcision was established as a sign to Abram and his seed that this symbol would be to remind them of the covenant that God had made with Abram. That being that through Abram, his seed would become a great nation. And that nation would become known as the nation of Israel. It is interesting that Ishmael was also circumcised, as well as anyone born into the house of Abram, including household workers or slaves that were bought with money.

Chapter 21 introduces us to the birth of Isaac. Abraham is now one hundred years old and Sarah ninety when Isaac was born. Ishmael was born outside of God's will for Abram. He was not the promised son. Genesis 21:12b says, "For in Isaac shall thy seed be called."

The Offering of Isaac

Can you imagine offering your son to die? Not only would that be difficult or impossible to do, but to actually kill him yourself? I can't imagine doing what God was asking Abraham to do here. Are you kidding me? Let's see, you gave me the son that you promised me and that through him you would build a nation of people, and now you want me to kill him. Are you sure? Are you nuts? How can a dead man have children?

That is what I would be thinking, I don't know about Abraham's thoughts, but what did he do? The Bible said that he trusted God.

It seems to me that God was asking a lot from Abraham. However, Abraham told Isaac that God would supply the sacrifice. On the surface we think that Abraham was trying not to alarm Isaac. But does it go deeper than that? Yes, Abraham believed God. This son of mine is to be offered to the Lord, and God said that he was the promised son that would continue my seed. If I follow God, and sacrifice Isaac, then God will raise him up again. I repeat: Abraham believed God.

Abraham rose up early in the morning and took his son Isaac, along with two of his young men, and traveled a three-day journey. He instructed his two men to wait for him there, and he and Isaac went up to the mountain to offer a sacrifice. Abraham loaded the wood on Isaac's back.

As the scene unfolds—as Abraham is about to take his son's life—an angel appears and stops him, and he sees a ram caught in a thicket of bushes. The ram becomes the sacrifice. God tested Abraham's faith that day. Abraham's faith was counted to him as righteousness. It is no different today. We are still saved by faith; our faith in the finished work of Christ is our righteousness.

As we ponder this and think about how hard this would be for us to do, God would do this very thing. As Isaac carried the wood, Christ would carry his cross. That ram in the thicket was a type of Christ—a forerunner of the Lamb of God. God would do the very thing that he stopped Abraham from doing. God would sacrifice his only begotten son on a cross at Calvary. He did this for you and me, and his son, Jesus, was more than willing to do so.

We are going to leave Abraham here, but before we move on there is something of interest here that I think a lot of people never think about. How many children did Abraham have? A lot of people believe that Isaac was an only child. They have never heard about nor read about Ishmael. If so, then they have probably not heard about Abraham's other six sons, and maybe you haven't either.

Abraham was eighty-six when Ishmael was born and one hundred when Isaac was born. Sarah died at the age of 127, and Abraham was ten years older. Two or three years later he married Keturah, and she gave birth to six sons. And now Abraham had eight sons, but it doesn't say anything about how many daughters he had—if any. He also had concubines, and they gave him more sons (Gen. 25:6). So we don't know how many children he had.

Esau and Jacob

Rebekah struggled with her pregnancy; she was about to give birth to twins. God revealed to her that she would have in her womb two nations (two manners of people). One stronger than the other, and the eldest would serve the younger.

One day Jacob was cooking some pottage; today we would call it bean soup. Esau had been out all day. He was the outdoor type: a man's man, rugged and physically strong. It was not unusual for him to be gone for long periods of time—often out hunting. Jacob, on the other hand, was more timid. Well let's call a spade a spade—he was a momma's boy.

Esau was very hungry, and he asked Jacob for some of his pottage, to which Jacob replied, "Sell me this day thy birthright." And Esau said, "Behold I am about to die, and what profit shall this birthright do me?" And Jacob said, "Swear to me this day," and he swore unto him, and he sold his birthright to Jacob.

Esau sold his birthright for a bowl of soup. I don't think that that is something to write home about. But get this: Adam sold the title deed to the earth for a piece of fruit. Now maybe you don't believe this, so let the scriptures speak on this.

> Again the devil, taketh him up into an exceeding high mountain, and sheweth him all the kingdoms of the world and the glory of them; And saith unto him, all these things will I give thee, if thou wilt fall down and worship me. (Matt. 4:8–9)

In 2 Corinthians 4:4 Paul calls Satan the god of this world. How could the devil, Satan, offer to give the whole world to Jesus if it were not his to give? In Ephesians 2:2 Paul calls Satan the prince and the power of the air, and in John 12:31 and 14:30 he calls him the prince of this world.

How did Satan get to be the prince and the power of the air and prince of this world? The dominion of the world was given to the man and woman that God created in the garden of eden.

> And God said, Let us make man in our image, after our likeness, and let them have dominion over the fish of the sea, and over the fowl of the air, and over cattle, and over all the earth, and over every creeping thing that creepeth upon the earth. So God created man in his own image, in the image of God created he him; male and female created he them. (Gen. 1:26–27)

> And the Lord God said unto the woman, what is this that thou hast done? And the woman said, the serpent beguiled me, and I did eat. (Gen. 3:13)

Because of the man and woman's sin (Adam and Eve), they gave up their rights to the serpent (Satan) and the dominion of the whole earth. So Adam sold the title deed of the earth. Satan tried to sell it back to Jesus, but Jesus did not like his terms. Jesus had terms of his own that he was not ready to divulge at this time; he would settle up with Satan later (Matt. 4:1–11).

In the book of Revelation we see Jesus standing and holding a scroll sealed with seven seals. This scroll is the title deed to the earth. How did he get it back from Satan? He bought it back. He paid the full ransom price for it—his death on the cross. Jesus paid it all. We no longer have a sin debt to pay.

Was Adam created in the garden of eden? No, not according to Genesis 2:8.

> And the Lord God planted a garden eastward in Eden; and there he put the man whom he had formed.

It sounds to me that man was made first, and then God placed him in the garden. So where was Adam created? I don't know, possibly somewhere west of the garden.

Moses

Moses was born a Hebrew but was raised in the palace of Pharaoh in Egypt. I'm sure that you are familiar about the baby Moses that was found in the bulrushes in the river, so we won't go into that. The children of Jacob ended up in Egypt because of a famine in Canaan. They were at first welcome there but later became slaves of the new Pharaoh. After 400 years, Moses comes on to the scene.

After Moses killed an Egyptian guard, he escaped into the desert. Forty years later, God reveals himself to Moses in a burning bush. God calls him to lead his people out of Egypt and into the Promised Land that had been promised to the seed of Abraham.

Moses delivers the Hebrews (Israelites) from Egypt, but because of their unbelief, they spent the next forty years in the wilderness, where Moses received the Ten Commandments from God. He built a tabernacle according to Gods explicit instructions. A tabernacle was a temporary house for God (a place where God would meet with the high priest). This tabernacle was the forerunner of the temple that would later be built in Jerusalem. All of the priests were to come from the tribe of Levi. The priest would sacrifice animals brought to them by the people for a sin offering.

The tabernacle was made up of three divisions. There was the outer court for the people, and the inner court was for the priest (this is where the alter of sacrifice was), and the third division was called the Holy of Holies, where only the high priest could enter once a year. In this third division is where they kept the Ark of the Covenant.

The high priest would sprinkle the blood of the animal onto the Ark of the Covenant for the nation of Israel for a sin offering. He would also sprinkle some blood on a live goat that would be led out into the wilderness and be left there with the sins of the people. This is called a scapegoat. Now you know where the term *scapegoat* comes from.

It is important to point out here that throughout the Old Testament, the blood of an animal was required to cover (or hide) sin. This ritual act could not remove sin, but it was an act that looked forward to the time when God would sacrifice his only begotten son, Jesus, on a cross at Calvary.

Here are some similarities between Jesus and Moses.

> Moses was the savior of the Hebrews.
> Jesus is the savior of all mankind.
> Both were born under unusual circumstances.
> Both escaped death as infants.
> Neither were accepted by their people.
> Both fasted for forty days.
> Both went up on a high mountain to pray.
> Both had angels attending their graves.
> Moses lifted up the serpent.
> Jesus was lifted up on a cross.
> They were both transfigured.

I find it fitting that Moses was one of the three that were transfigured as witnessed by Peter, James, and John. The three that were transfigured were Jesus, Moses, and Elijah.

We are going to fast-forward now in the next chapter to the New Testament. My intent here was to give the reader some background information on

Israel, not to enlighten one on all scripture. It would be good, however, to read the entire Bible cover to cover as a book because it contains the entire history of God's dealing with mankind.

Before we get to the next chapter, I wanted to cover a very important aspect of the Bible, and that is the meaning and the use of numbers. Here is a list of numbers and examples of uses.

1. Unity – One body, one Spirit, one Lord, one Father
2. Union – Marriage, Christ and the church, Noah's ark 2 x 2, two tablets of stone, two witnesses
3. Divinity – Trinity of God, of man, Christ tempted three times, arose from the tomb on the third day
4. Worldly – Four seasons, four points on the compass, four cherubims, four faces, four wings, four corners of the earth
5. Division or Grace–Five wise and five foolish virgins, five loaves of bread, feeding five thousand
6. Man – Six days of creation in Genesis, man created on the sixth day, work six days, six-day march on Jericho, Man's number is 6
7. God's number of completion or perfection – The Sabbath on the seventh day, seven days in

a week, Enoch seventh from Adam, seven-day grace period on the ark

8. New order of beginnings–Eighth day starts a new week, Circumcised on the eighth day, eight souls saved on the ark

10. Worldly completion – Ten Commandments, ten toes, ten horns, ten virgins

12. Eternal perfection – Twelve sons, twelve tribes, twelve gates of pearl, twelve angels, twelve disciples

40. Probation or testing – Forty-day flood, Nineveh given forty days to repent, Elijah fasted for forty days, Christ tempted by Satan after forty days of fasting

As you read the Bible, you will notice these numbers often, especially the numbers 7 and 40.

As you read the Old Testament, notice that the church age is absent. It is absent because God has kept it hidden from the prophets. The Jews as a nation are still waiting for the Messiah to come and to set up his kingdom. They have rejected Jesus as the Messiah. The mystery of the church was revealed to Paul after his conversion on the road to Damascus.

The Trinity of God

God the Father
God the Son
God the Holy Spirit

These three make up the Godhead. All three are separate in function and personage. Yet they are all one. How can one explain this? I don't know that it can be explained; we are to take God at his word and believe it to be so. I can, however, give you an example that might help.

My name is Don. I am a person that you can see, talk to, and interact with if you so choose. Yet you cannot see all of me. You can only see my body. What you can't see is my soul and spirit. The soul and spirit help define who I am. All three parts of me are different with different functions, yet they are all me.

Spirit and Soul

The spirit is the part that has fellowship with God.

The soul is our personality. It is who we are, made up of mind, will, and emotions.

Alpha and Omega

When Jesus said, "I am the Alpha and Omega," he was saying that with him and through him, all things began and will end with him. We often think of this as a timeline.

Alpha——————————————————Omega
Beginning Ending

But think of a circle rather than a straight line.
Alpha and Omega as being at any spot on that circle.
Christ will return things to the beginning.

Alpha and Omega

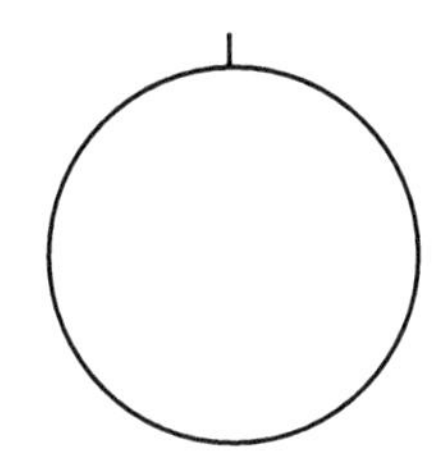

Genesis (Alpha)	Revelation (Omega)
God made the sun and moon.	God did away with them
God created heaven and earth.	God made new ones.
Kept Adam and Eve from the tree of life.	Welcomes us to eat from the tree.
Created the seas.	No more seas.
Dark 50% of the time.	No more darkness.
The first wedding.	The last wedding.
Always thirsty.	Thirsty nevermore.
Ground cursed because of sin.	Curse removed.

The Bible, as well as time, has a beginning and an ending, bringing us right back to the beginning.

At the end of chapter 1 I asked a question. What do the first two chapters and the last two chapters of the Bible have in common? It is not what you read in these chapters but what you do not read. There is something missing from these four chapters. The answer is sin. Actually, to be correct, it is the absence of sin. The first two chapters of Genesis is before sin, and the last two chapters of Revelation are after sin has been abolished. This brings us right back to the beginning. Isn't it amazing how God looks after every detail in the Bible?

4

The New Testament

Matthew starts with the genealogy of Jesus starting with Abraham; actually, this is the genealogy of Joseph. The genealogy of Mary is found in Luke 3:23–38. These two genealogies going back to King David are different. Joseph is a descendent of David's son Solomon. Mary is a descendent of David's son Nathan. Joseph's ancestry goes back to Abraham, and Mary's goes back to Adam, the son of God.

As I was reviewing these scriptures, I noticed something that I have never noticed before. I have read this many times before, and I know about the fourteen generations, but I never gave it much thought until now, and I wondered, how long is a generation?

> So all the generations from Abraham to David are fourteen generations; and from David until the carrying away into Babylon are fourteen generations; and from the carrying away into Babylon unto Christ are fourteen generations. (Matt. 1:17)

> Verily I say unto you, this generation shall not pass till all these things be fulfilled. (Matt. 24:34)

In Matthew 24 the disciples asked Jesus when the end will come and what were the signs of his coming. The whole chapter is devoted to the end of time as we know it.

In Matthew 1:17 there are three sets of fourteen generations (3 x 14 = 42 generations) covering a period of two thousand years from Abraham until Christ. In order to determine how long a generation was, we simply divide the length of time by the number of generations, and that gives us an average of forty-five years per generation.

The nation of Israel was scattered abroad in all nations in 70 AD when Titus, a Roman general, defeated Israel and demolished the city of Jerusalem and the temple. In 1948 Israel gained recognition as a state, but they did not have control of Jerusalem until after the Six-Day War in 1967.

If this is the generation that Christ was referring to in Matthew 24:34, starting from 1967, add one generation of forty-five years, and you get the year 2012. I'm not trying to set a date here, but I find it interesting when you hear of the Mayan calendar that ends on December 21, 2012. And at this winter solstice, according to astronomers, the sun will be aligned with the center of our galaxy, the Milky Way. Interesting, but it didn't happen.

No one knows the day or the hour, not even Jesus, but we are told about what to expect in the realm of prophecies about the end of time.

> But of that day and hour knoweth no man, no, not the angels of heaven, but my Father only. But as the days of Noe were so shall also the coming of the Son of man be. (Matt. 24:36–37)

The Birth of Jesus

Luke 2:1–7 gives us the account of the birth of Jesus. Why did God choose Mary to be the mother of Jesus? There must have been a number of virgin girls in Israel at that time, so why Mary? Well for the same reason that he chose Noah, Moses, Abraham, the disciples, Paul, and many others. And what is that reason? Because God in his foreknowledge knew that they were willing. He wouldn't call someone if they were not willing to do what God had in store for them.

> And Mary said, Behold the handmaid of the Lord; be it unto me according to thy word. (Luke 1:38)

Even though she could be subject to ridicule and scorn, even the possibility of being stoned to death, she was willing, and she had faith in God. What would Joseph think about this situation? How would you feel if your wife-to-be was pregnant and you knew that the child was not yours? Fear not, God has a plan as usual.

> Now the birth of Jesus was on this wise: When as his mother Mary was espoused to Joseph, before they had come together, she was found with child of the Holy Ghost. Then Joseph her husband, being a just man, and not willing to make her a public example, was minded to put her away privily. But while he thought on these things, behold, the angel of the Lord appeared unto him in a dream saying, Joseph, thou son of David, fear not to take unto thee Mary thy wife: for that which is conceived in her is of the Holy Spirit. And she shall bring forth a son, and thou shalt call his name Jesus: for he shall save his people from their sins. (Matt. 1:18–21)

Now skip to verse 24: "Then Joseph being raised from sleep did as the angel of the Lord had bidden him, and took unto him his wife."

Now for a word on the culture at that time. A wedding ceremony was not a one-hour deal. There was time to get to know each other and family. Time for the husband to prepare a home for his wife. Time to earn and pay a dowry to her family, if required. This marriage could take a long time, often a full year. The marriage was not complete until it was consummated by their coming together. During all this time they are married. The wedding feast itself might last a week. Then the husband and wife would consummate the marriage by sleeping together. Joseph and Mary did not consummate their marriage until after the birth of Jesus.

> And knew her not till she had brought forth her first born son: and he called his name JESUS. (Matt. 1:25)

We are going to transition here so I can explain the difference between what Christ was teaching the Jews under the law and what Paul was teaching the Gentiles under grace. It is very important to understand these differences and to keep them in their proper place as you read the Bible.

Paul was called by Jesus to be an apostle to the Gentiles because the twelve disciples did not go out into the world as they were commanded to do in Matthew 28:19, Mark 16:15, Luke 24:47, and Acts 1:8. They stayed in Jerusalem.

You are either a Jew or a Gentile; simply put, we are all Gentiles unless we are Jewish. Other names for Gentiles are, to name a few, uncircumcised, Greeks, ungodly, heathens, and dogs. There may be more that I can't think of right now. When you remove Paul's epistles from the Bible, you also remove the church. And you are left with a Bible that is strictly for the Jews. Paul's epistles are written to the true church, also known as the body of Christ. You cannot mix the two—the Jews under the law and the body of Christ under grace.

I am a member of the body of Christ, therefore I am attuned to Paul's writings. The rest of the Bible is for my learning and understanding. Without the rest of the Bible, there would be nothing but chaos for the church. If you read Paul's epistles, they wouldn't be of much benefit without the background of information contained in the rest of the Bible.

From Adam to Abraham, everyone was a Gentile for two thousand years. From Abraham came the Jewish nation of Israel, and they had been prominent until Christ's death, burial, and resurrection—another two thousand years. Ushering in the body of Christ that has lasted now for nearly two thousand years. Next, and I think very soon, will come the return of Christ and the one-thousand-year kingdom that the Jews are waiting and longing for.

This makes up seven thousand years of mankind. The earth and man were created in six days, and God rested on the seventh day. There has been six thousand years since Adam, and then man and the earth will rest for one thousand years. The number 7 is God's number of perfection and completeness. From Adam to the cross was a dispensation of law. From the cross until the rapture of the church is the dispensation of grace.

Why was the law given to the Jews? It was not given to them for salvation. It was given to show their guilt of sin so that they would turn to God.

> Now we know that what things soever the law saith, it saith to them who are under the law; that every mouth may be stopped, and all the world may become guilty before God. Therefore by the deeds of the law there shall no flesh be justified in his sight; for by the law is the knowledge of sin. (Rom. 3:19–20)

Jesus: Minister of the Jews

> But when the fullness of the time was come, God sent forth his Son, made of a woman, made under the law. To redeem them that were under the law, that we might receive the adoption of sons. (Gal. 4:4–5)

> And she shall bring forth a son, and thou shalt call his name JESUS: for he shall save his people from their sins. (Matt. 1:21)

The Jews were under the dispensation of law, therefore Jesus was a Jew under the law. Why did he come to earth? To redeem us? Are we under the law? No. He came to earth to redeem them that were under the law, to save his people (the Jews) from their sins. Did this happen? No. Only a remnant were saved. People flocked to him, not for salvation, but they came to him because of his miracles. As a nation they rejected him and crucified him, led by the keepers of the law, the Pharisees and the Sadducees, the religious rulers of the time.

Christ brought salvation to the Gentiles through Paul because the Jews as a whole had rejected him. Paul started Gentile churches outside of Israel, mostly in Asia Minor, which is now Turkey. Paul was the apostle to the Gentiles, yet he also preached to the Jews that were scattered abroad. Paul states in Galatians 4:5 that we might receive the adoption of sons. What does he mean *we*, and *adoption*? We are the members of the body of Christ, and we have been grafted in, or adopted, because of the Jews' unbelief.

> I say then, Have they stumbled that they should fall? God forbid: but rather through their fall salvation is come unto the Gentiles, for to provoke them to jealousy. (Rom. 11:11)

> For I speak to you Gentiles, inasmuch as I am the apostle of the Gentiles, I magnify mine office. If by any means I may provoke to emulation them which are my flesh, and might save some of them. (Rom. 11:13–14)

Paul was sent by Jesus to the Gentiles. Why? To provoke the Jews to jealousy. Paul was writing to the Gentile church in Galatia. In verse 13 he is speaking to the Gentiles; notice also in this verse that Paul says, "I am *the* apostle to the Gentiles," not *an* apostle. In verse 14 he states "them which are my flesh." Paul was a Jew; he was reiterating the fact that the Jews are his kin.

Most believers think that Jesus came to earth to save all sinners. But this is not what scripture says to me. And most would use a scripture reference like this one:

> For the Son of man is come to save that which was lost. (Matt. 18:11)

This is a good example of quoting scripture out of context. On the surface this seems to include every one. But first notice that he said "was lost," not "are lost." So this does not include the body of Christ. Now when we look at verse 1, he is talking to the disciples, not the body of Christ. In verse 17 he is talking about the church, but this is not the true church the body of Christ). This is an assembly or ecclesia. Now go back and read Galatians 4:4–5 again. Why did Jesus come? To redeem (or save) them that were under the Law. The body of Christ is not under the law. I am a member of the body of Christ; I am not under the law, but I have been saved by God's grace. In Matthew 10:5–7 Jesus calls his twelve disciples together and sends them out to preach.

> These twelve Jesus sent forth, and commanded them, saying, Go not into the way of the Gentiles, and into any city of the Samaritans enter ye not. But go rather to the lost sheep of the house of Israel. And as ye go preach, saying, The kingdom of heaven is at hand (Matt. 10:5–7).

> But he answered and said, I am not sent but unto the lost sheep of the house of Israel. (Matt. 15:24)

> Him hath God exaulted with his right hand to be a Prince and a Savior for to give repentance to Israel, and forgiveness of sins. (Acts 5:31)

Nowhere in the Bible is the body of Christ (known as the true church) called sheep. I am a member of the body of Christ, therefore He is not my shepherd. I might also add that Jesus is the king of the Jews, not king of the church; therefore, he is not my king. He is my Lord and savior. In Revelation, he is seen as the King of kings and Lord of lords—Israel's King and our Lord.

Remember Galatians 4:4–5? Jesus was a Jew made of a woman under the law to redeem them that were under the law. In his first dispensation, he did not come to the church; he came for his own, Israel.

Jesus was a Jew, brought up under the law, lived by the law, and taught according to the law. He did not preach, nor did he fellowship with anyone except Jews. There are, however, two incidences where he dealt with Gentiles, Matthew 15:21–28 and Matthew 8:5–13, and both were for healing, not salvation.

In chapter 15 Jesus deals with a Syrophenician woman, a Greek (Mark 7:26). She called out to him saying, "Have mercy on me, O Lord, thou son of David." Here we have a non-Jew addressing Jesus as the son of David. Only a Jew could address another Jew in such a way. Therefore Jesus does not answer her. He later refers to her as a dog. The disciples want Jesus to send her away. Again Jesus states that he has come only for the lost sheep of the house of Israel.

Then she worships him as Lord saying, help me. Jesus then replies to her, saying that it is not good to take the children's (Jews') bread and feed it to the dogs (Gentiles). Jesus then meets her request. Because of her faith, her daughter is healed.

In chapter 8 Jesus deals with a Roman centurion. The man addressed Jesus as Lord; therefore, Jesus listens to the man's plea for healing of his servant. Jesus commends his faith and the servant is healed. I don't know if this has any significance or not, but I noticed that they both sought Jesus on someone else's behalf and not for themselves. She for her daughter and he for his servant.

Jesus was not sent to minister to the Gentiles; he came only to the Jews—with some exceptions. And what were these Jews to believe? That Jesus was the son of God, the Christ (Messiah).

> When Jesus came into the coasts of Caesarea Philippe, he asked his disciples, saying, Whom do men say that I the Son of man am? And they said, some say that thou art John the Baptist: some Elias; and others, Jeramias, or one of the prophets. He saith unto them, But whom say ye that I am? And Simon Peter answered and said, Thou art the Christ, the Son of the living God. (Matt. 16:13–16)

In John 11 Jesus comes to the tomb of Lazarus, a good friend that had recently died.

> Then said Martha unto Jesus, Lord, if thou hadst been here, my brother had not died. But I know, that even now, whatsoever thou wilt ask of God, God will give it thee. Jesus saith unto her, Thy brother shall rise again. Martha saith unto him, I know that he shall rise again in the resurrection at the last day. Jesus said unto her, I am the resurrection, and the life, he that

> believeth in me, though he were dead, yet shall he live. And whosoever liveth and believeth in me shall never die. Believest thou this? She saith unto him, Yea, Lord, I believe that thou art the Christ, the Son of God, which should come into the world. (John 11:21–27)

Did she or Peter believe in the death burial and resurrection of Christ like Christians believe? No, of course not; this hasn't happened yet. The Jews were simply to believe that Jesus was who he said that he was, and that is all that they were to believe for their salvation. Jesus is God.

That was the system or dispensation of the Jews under the law. We, the body of Christ, are also to believe that Jesus is God and that he died, was buried, and has risen. His death as the sacrificial lamb, his shed blood for the remission of sin, and his resurrection seals our fate that we also will be resurrected. This is the dispensation of grace.

Jesus brought salvation to the Jews under the law if they believed in him. Paul brought salvation to the Gentiles if they believed in the death, burial, and resurrection of Jesus. Two different dispensations, so don't mix them. You have to keep this in mind, or you will get them mixed. Remember, oil and water do not mix. Keep things in their proper place.

Isaiah, a Jewish prophet, writes in Isaiah 9:6: "For unto us [the Jews] a child is born [Jesus], unto us [the Jews] a son [Jesus] is given."

Jesus was born for the salvation of Israel, not for the body of Christ; however, Israel rejected Jesus as the Christ (Messiah), and we, the body of Christ, have been grafted in.

We are now in a different dispensation of time, which started after the death of Jesus. His death, burial and resurrection ended the dispensation of law. When Christ died, the veil of the temple was torn in two from the top to the bottom, ending the dispensation of law. We can now come to God personally without going to the high priest as Israel had to do because Jesus became the high priest for the whole human race. We can now go directly to the throne of grace. We do not have to offer sacrifices because Jesus is our sacrificial lamb. He died once for all whereas the Jews, under the law, sacrificed animals weekly, monthly, and yearly.

You may have noticed by now how often I repeat some things. That is because I feel it is important. Therefore, I may repeat some things often. Familiarity brings remembrance. I want you to get the point.

5

The Apostle Paul

Saul was a Jewish leader, most likely a member of the Sanhedrin, which is much like our Senate but was a religious group. He was absolutely opposed to the new church that was being formed by Peter and the other disciples. This group (ecclesiastical) believed that Jesus was the son of God. This caused a serious problem for Saul and the other Pharisees. Saul was a staunch believer in the Torah and a strict keeper of the law. He had taken it upon himself to also be an enforcer of the law.

Saul, later to become known as Paul, was first introduced at the stoning of Stephen. Acts 7 tells the story of Stephen and how the witnesses and partakers in the stoning laid their coats at Saul's feet.

> And Saul was consenting unto his death. And at that time there was a great persecution against the church which was at Jerusalem; and they were all scattered abroad throughout the regions of Judea and Samaria, except for the apostles. And devout men carried Stephen

> to his burial, and made great lamentation over him. As for Saul, he made havoc of the church, entering into every house, and haling men and women committed them to prison. (Acts 8:1–3)

The citizens of Jerusalem were, for the most part, religious and lived according to the law of Moses as much as they could. And Saul was a much-admired leader that commanded a lot of respect because of his dedication to the cause—the cause being that there was a religious difference between the ruling party in Jerusalem and this new church. Saul was on a mission to bring these believers, who were scattered abroad throughout Judea, back to Jerusalem to be imprisoned for their belief. They were often put to death.

Saul's Conversion

> And Saul, yet breathing out threatenings and slaughter against the disciples of the Lord went unto the high priest, And desired of him letters to Damascus to the synagogues, that if he found any of this way, whether they were men or women, he might bring them bound unto Jerusalem. And as he journeyed, he came near Damascus; and suddenly there shined round about him a light from heaven; And he fell to the earth, and heard a voice saying unto him, Saul, Saul, why persecutest thou me? And he said, Who art thou, Lord? And the Lord said, I am Jesus whom thou persecutest: it is

> hard for thee to kick against the pricks. And he trembling and astonished said, Lord, what wilt thou have me to do? And the Lord said unto him, arise, and go into the city, and it shall be told thee what thou must do. And the men which journeyed with him stood speechless, hearing a voice, but seeing no man. And Saul arose from the earth; and when his eyes were opened, he saw no man: but they led him by the hand, and brought him unto Damascus. And he was three days without sight, and neither did eat nor drink. (Acts 9:1–9)

If you are without Christ in your life as Saul was, even though he was a religious zealot, you may feel that you are doing just fine on your own or that you are so vile and wicked that you cannot be saved. Well think again. If Jesus was willing to save Saul, someone that did all he could to keep people from their belief that Jesus was the Christ, why do you feel that he couldn't save you? In fact, God is not willing that any should perish but that all should come to repentance.

God wants to save you and give you a new life. God is willing; how about you? Are you ready to receive Jesus right now? God's plan for salvation is simple: believe and receive—that's it. What am I to believe, and how do I receive? Faith is the key to everything with God. Without faith, it is impossible to please God.

> That if thou shalt confess with the mouth the Lord Jesus and shalt Believe in thine heart that

> God hath raised him from the dead, thou shalt be saved. For with the heart man believeth unto righteousness; and with the mouth confession is made unto salvation. (Rom. 10:9–10)

If you believe that Jesus is the son of God and that he came to earth and was crucified, buried, and rose again the third day to pay the penalty for your sins, and you feel the Spirit of God in your heart, then it is time for you to receive. Just ask Jesus to come into your heart and life, and he will. That's it.

It is so unbelievably simple. Yet so many people think that they have to do something to deserve his forgiveness. It could be that you are worried about what others might think. Who cares? This is important to you—a life-or-death decision. Jesus' death = your life.

Some people believe that because Jesus died once for all and that he paid the penalty for all sin, past, present, and future, everyone will go to heaven. Part of this is true. Jesus did die once for all, and he did pay the penalty for all sin past, present, and future. But everyone does not go to heaven even though their sin debt has been paid. Only those that accept the finished work of the cross personally will go to heaven. God created man for fellowship. He wants to interact with those that choose him. Therefore, he gave us the freedom of choice. You can go to heaven and be with God, or you can go to hell and be with Satan. It's your choice.

God could have made us in such a way that we would all love him and follow his commands, but he didn't—he already has the angels in heaven to do that. When you receive Christ as your personal savior, you immediately become a child of God and joint heirs with Christ. But if you do not accept Jesus, then you will remain a child of Satan.

Jesus calls the scribes and Pharisees the children of the devil.

> Ye are of your father the Devil, and the lusts of your father ye will do. (John 8:44)

Now turn your Bible to Matthew 23 and read it completely. Notice how often Jesus denounces the Scribes and the Pharisees. These are the wealthy religious rulers, the law keepers.

Were these people any different than we are today? Probably not. Our different denominations of churches are diversified. Each one believing that theirs is the best. They each have laws, or maybe we choose to call them suggestions, on how we should live. No smoking, no alcohol, no dancing, etc. They also have certain expectations: Come to church at least three times a week, give of your time to the church, and tithe at least ten percent plus offerings. Does this sound like your church? Does this put us right back where the Pharisees were—under the law?

Did you know that tithing was a Jewish law? It was not intended for the church, the body of Christ. Nowhere in Paul's epistles does he even hint at tithing.

And why doesn't he? It's because we are no longer under the law of Moses that the Jews were under. Paul's epistles are to the seven churches that are mostly in Asia Minor and Rome. They are predominately Gentiles. He talks about tithing in Hebrews 7, but this book is written to the Jews under the law. Verse 5 says to take tithes of the people according to the law.

The majority of Paul's epistles to these churches are written to give instructions on how to conduct themselves and to explain the mysteries that God revealed to him. He does not instruct them to tithe, but he does say that they should be self-supporting and that the people should give as the Holy Spirit leads them.

I am not saying that it is wrong to tithe. If God leads you to tithe, then by all means you should do so. I just want you to know that it is not a requirement. If your church requires you to tithe, well they shouldn't, unless of course you are a Jew in a synagogue.

Just remember, all you have to do is believe and receive. Jesus did the rest. End of story. Jesus died for all, but you have to be proactive in that you must believe that he died for you. You cannot sit on the fence on this. You have to make a choice. You cannot be passive. To do so means that you do not want to make a choice. If so, then you have already made a decision not to follow Christ. Let me give you an example.

It's Christmas Eve, you have spent all of your money on gifts for your children, and you realize that you haven't gotten anything for your wife. There is a man standing on the corner in front of the jewelry store, and he is passing out one-hundred-dollar bills to anyone that wants one. He is a very rich man, and he has plenty of money to give. He wants to give back to the community that helped him become a rich man. You walk up to him, reach out your hand, and take one. You thank him, and then you go into the jewelry store and buy a gift for your wife.

Another man is offered a one-hundred-dollar bill, but the man does not take the money. Oh, he may have several reasons for not taking the money such as, "I think he is running for public office. and he is trying to buy my vote," or he may be thinking, "I don't need your money, I can get by on my own."

The money is there for you if you want it, but the rich man cannot force you to take it. But the thing is—and this is very important—you cannot get the benefit of the money if you don't reach out and accept it. Reach out to Jesus now before it is too late.

Paul to the Gentiles

The conversion of Paul is recorded in Acts 9. The book of Acts is a transitional book. It takes the reader from the Jews under the law to the Gentiles under grace.

> Then Ananias answered, Lord, I have heard by many of this man, how much evil he hath done to thy saints at Jerusalem. And here he hath authority from the chief priests to bind all that call on thy name. But the Lord said unto him,

> Go thy way: for he is a chosen vessel unto me, to bear my name before the Gentiles, and kings, and the children of Israel. (Acts 9:13–15)

Christ spent three years with the disciples, and they were converting the Jews in Jerusalem. But here Christ calls out Saul of Tarsus to take the gospel to the Gentiles.

Paul and Barnabas were being confronted by the Jews of the church in Jerusalem, because they were preaching to the Gentiles.

> And the next Sabbath day came almost the whole city together to hear the word of God. But when the Jews saw the multitudes, they were filled with envy, and spake against those things which were spoken by Paul, contradicting and blaspheming. Then Paul and Barnabas waxed bold, and, said It was necessary that the word of God should first have been spoken to you [the Jews], but seeing ye put it from you, and judge yourselves unworthy of everlasting life, Lo, we turn to the Gentiles. (Acts 13:44–46)

Paul has been trying to make some progress with the Jews but is now tiring of their rejection.

> And he reasoned in the synagogue every Sabbath, and persuaded the Jews and the Greeks. And when Silas and Timotheus were come from Macedonia, Paul was pressed in the spirit, and testified to the Jews that Jesus was

> Christ. And when they opposed themselves, and blasphemed, he shook his raiment, and said unto them. Your blood be upon your own heads, I am clean: from henceforth I will go unto the Gentiles. (Acts 18:4–6)

Paul was a religious Jew steeped in the law. At this point in time he had not yet been shown the mystery of the body of Christ, the true church. That will come after he spends three years in Arabia, probably at Mt. Sinai. Jesus spent three years with the disciples, and now he will spend three years with Paul. All that Paul was preaching now was that Jesus is the Christ.

When Jesus was with his disciples, he sent them out to reach others (Matt. 10:5–6). He told them not to go to the Gentiles but only to the lost sheep of the house of Israel. But when Christ was crucified, buried, and resurrected, the veil of the temple was rent into from the top to the bottom, ending the dispensation of law. He told them in Mark 16:15 to go into all the world and preach the gospel to every creature. Did they do that? No. They stayed in Jerusalem. Read about Peter's vision in Acts 10 about the sheet being let down from heaven containing what Peter called unclean food.

Peter was given a vision, and because of this vision he went to the house of Cornelius, a Gentile. After Peter preached to the household of Cornelius, they became believers in Christ and were baptized. But Peter went right back to Jerusalem and stayed there with the other disciples. They did not go out into the world to preach the gospel as God had told them to do. So God called Paul to do what the disciples would not do. Later, when Paul was confronting the Jewish church on the subject of circumcision and the law, Peter remembered that God had saved Gentiles through his dealing with the household of Cornelius, and he spoke up in Paul's defense.

> But there rose up certain of the sect of the Pharisees which believed, saying, That it was needful to circumcise them, and to command them to keep the law of Moses. And the apostles and elders came together for to consider of this matter. (Acts 15:5–6)

These Jewish Christians are not the true church (the body of Christ). The church in the early chapters of Acts, where the three thousand were saved, still felt it necessary to be circumcised and to keep the law of Moses according to verse 5 above. They were believers. I know that this is not what most people have been taught, and it might be hard to understand. The twelve disciples, now apostles, and the elders still held on to the law of Moses. We the body of Christ are not under the burden of the law but are under the freedom of God's grace. Keep this in mind as you read and study your Bible, and it will make more sense to you.

> And when there had been much disputing, Peter rose up, and said unto them, Men and brethren, ye know how that a good while ago God made choice among us, that the Gentiles by my mouth should hear the word of the gospel, and believe.

> And God which knoweth the hearts, bare them witness, giving them the Holy Ghost, even as he did unto us; And put no difference between us and them, purifying their hearts by faith. Now therefore why tempt ye God, to put a yoke upon the neck of the disciples, which neither our fathers nor we were able to bear? But we believe that through the grace of the Lord Jesus Christ we shall be saved, even as they. (Acts 15:7–11)

Peter confirms that the converts of Paul are not under the law but are saved by the grace of God. Abraham was called by God to be the father of the Jewish nation of Israel. Moses was called by God to deliver his people from Egypt. We read of this, and we believe it to be true. But when we read that Jesus came to earth to be the savior of his people, the nation of Israel, we don't believe this. We choose to believe that he came to build his church (the body of Christ). This church is the result of the Jews' rejection of their Messiah, Jesus. Paul was called by God because the eleven disciples that were to go into all the world and preach the gospel did not go; they chose to stay in Jerusalem. Most Christians do not understand this; why can't we get this straight? Christ was sent to Israel, Paul was sent to the Gentiles.

After this meeting that Paul and Barnabas had with the church in Jerusalem, they went on their way to continue preaching Jesus to the Gentiles.

Paul's Mysteries

What is a mystery in biblical terms? A mystery is a secret concealed in God until it is revealed at a time of his choosing. Here are two of the mysteries that were revealed to Paul concerning the true church.

> For this cause I Paul, the prisoner of Jesus Christ for you Gentiles. If you have heard of the dispensation of the grace of God which is given me to you -ward. How that by revelation he made known unto me the mystery (as I wrote afore in few words. Whereby, when ye read, ye may understand my knowledge in the mystery of Christ.) (Eph. 3:1–4)

So what is the mystery of Christ?

> Whereof I am made a minister, according to the dispensation of God which is given to me for you, to fulfill the word of God. Even the mystery which hath been hid from ages and generations, but now is made manifest to his saints. To whom God would make known what is the riches of the glory of this mystery among the Gentiles; which is Christ in you, the hope of glory (Col. 1:25–27).

> That their hearts might be comforted, being knit together in love, and unto all riches of the full assurance of understanding to the acknowledgement of the mystery of God, and of the Father, and of Christ. In whom are hid all

> the treasures of wisdom and knowledge. (Col. 2:2–3)

I use a Scofield Reference Bible, and I like this footnote. The mystery of God is Christ, as incarnating the fullness of the Godhead and all the divine wisdom and knowledge for the redemption and reconciliation of man.

Here we have the revealing of the true church, the body of Christ. The next, and very important, mystery or secret is found in 1 Thessalonians and 1Corinthians, and that is we shall not all die if we are alive when Christ returns for the true church, the body of Christ. This is referred to as the rapture. The word *rapture* is not in the Bible, but the events that will occur are referred to as the rapture. So if I use the word *rapture*, it will be referring to the calling out of the body of Christ at His return.

> But I would not have you to be ignorant, brethren, concerning them which are asleep, that ye sorrow not, even as others which have no hope. For if we believe that Jesus died and rose again, even so them also which sleep in Jesus will God bring with him. For this we say unto you by the word of the Lord, that we which are alive and remain unto the coming of the Lord shall not prevent them which are asleep. For the Lord himself shall descend from heaven with

> a shout, with the voice of the Archangel, and with the trump of God, and the dead in Christ shall rise first. Then we which are alive and remain shall be caught up together with them in the clouds, to meet the Lord in the air: and so shall we ever be with the Lord. Wherefore comfort one another with these words. (1 Thess. 4:13–18)

Please, whenever you are reading the Bible, find out who is writing the scripture and to whom is it being written. For instance, this is Paul, the apostle, writing to the church in Thessalonica, a local church that is a part of the body of Christ. Verse 16 says those that are dead in Christ—that is, those that have received Christ for salvation that are now dead. Then verse 17 includes those that are alive when Christ returns. Notice also that verse 17 starts with, "Then we." Paul is including himself here, expecting Jesus to return in his lifetime.

I am expecting the Lord to return soon. I am ready, how about you? Are you ready to meet your maker? My prayer is that you are ready, and if you are not, then I pray that you will give your heart to Jesus now.

> Behold, I show you a mystery; we shall not all sleep, but we shall all be changed, In a moment, in the twinkling of an eye, at the last trump: For the trumpet shall sound, and the dead shall be raised incorruptible, and we shall be changed. For this corruptible must put on incorruption, and this mortal must put on immortality.

> So when this corruptible shall have put on incorruption, and this mortal shall have put on immortality, then shall be brought to pass the saying that is written, Death is swallowed up in victory. (1 Cor. 15:51–54)

As a part of the body of Christ, we will receive a new body, one that will not decay or get old. Even a genius uses less than 10% of his brain capacity; imagine what it would be like to use 100%. And have a new body that will last forever.

The Gospel

What is the gospel that Paul speaks of when he says "my gospel?" First, we will look at some scriptures where he says "my gospel."

> In the day when God shall judge the secrets of men by Jesus Christ according to my gospel (Rom. 2:16).

> Now to him that is of power to establish you according to my gospel and the preaching of Jesus Christ, according to the revelation of the mystery, which was kept secret since the world began (Rom. 16:25).

> Remember that Jesus Christ of the seed of David was raised from the dead according to my gospel (2 Tim. 2:8).

The gospel that Paul is calling my gospel is found in 1Corinthians 15:1–4:

> More over brethren I declare unto you the gospel which I preached unto you, which also ye have received, and wherein you stand, By which also ye are saved, if ye keep in memory what I preached unto you, unless ye have believed in vain. For I delivered unto you first of all that which I also received, how that Christ died for our sins according to the scriptures; And that he was buried, and that he rose again the third day according to the scriptures.

Herein is the gospel of grace. That Jesus died for our sins, was buried, and rose again to enable those that love him to have eternal life with him.

6

Other Important Subjects

Jesus Foretells of His Death, Burial, and Resurrection

The disciples loved Jesus, and they believed that he was the son of God, the much-awaited Messiah. Jesus told his disciples of his impending death and resurrection, but they did not understand how Jesus, the son of God, could die. Was this not the Messiah that was promised to Israel? The disciples were expecting that Jesus would set up his kingdom now.

> From that time forth began Jesus to shew unto his disciples, how that he must go unto Jerusalem, and suffer many things of the elders and chief priests and scribes, and be killed, and be raised again the third day. (Matt. 16:21)
>
> And while they abode in Galilee, Jesus said unto them, The Son of man shall be betrayed unto the hands of men; And they shall kill him,

> and the third day he shall be raised again. And they were exceedingly sorry. (Matt. 17:22–23)
>
> For he taught his disciples, and said unto them, The Son of man is delivered into the hands of men, and they shall kill him and after that he is killed, he shall rise the third day. But they understood not that saying, and were afraid to ask him. (Mark 9:31–32)
>
> Then he took unto him, the twelve, and said unto them, Behold we go up to Jerusalem, and all things that are written by the prophets concerning the Son of Man shall be accomplished. For he shall be delivered unto the Gentiles, and shall be mocked, and spitefully entreated, and spitted on: And they shall scourge him and put him to death; and the third day he shall rise again. And they understood none of these things, and this saying was hid from them, neither knew they the things which were spoken. (Luke 18:31–34)

I think that you get the point. The disciples did not know of Jesus's death, burial, and resurrection. They were told and they should have known, but they didn't. And why didn't they know? Because it was hidden from them by God. Had they understood this, they would probably have tried to stop this from happening. That would not be a good thing. It was necessary that Jesus fulfill his mission.

If you were one of the disciples, would you be gathered together with the others in an upper room on resurrection morning if you knew that Jesus would rise from the grave on that morning? I don't know about you, but I would be waiting at the tomb.

God Does Not Make Mistakes

I will use my son Norman here as an example. I trust that Norman will not mind my using him for an example. Norman was born with spina bifida, a spinal cord deficiency. He was born with a hole in his lower back, and he also has a shunt in his head. A shunt is a type of valve that drains excess fluid from the brain. Norman is handicapped, but he doesn't want to be treated in any special way. He doesn't think of himself as being handicapped, and neither do I because God doesn't make mistakes.

Can God heal Norman? Yes, of course he can, but he will not because as I just said, God does not make mistakes. Norman would not be Norman if he were not handicapped. He would be different. He is just exactly how God planned for him to be. He is perfect in God's eyes.

To further explain this, I will use myself as an example (I have my permission). My mother was from a Pennsylvania Dutch family that lived in a small community in western Pennsylvania. Around the turn of the twentieth century, my father's family moved from Austria and settled in that same western valley in Pennsylvania. My parents met, fell in love, got married, and had five children. I was number 4.

God released an egg from my mother, and not just any egg, but a particular egg. And from my father's sperm, God chose one particular spermatozoa and empowered it to swim ahead to fertilize that egg. Now get this. God knew me before the foundation of the earth. Any other egg or spermatozoa, and it would not have been me. Maybe my sister or brother, but it would not be me. I—or Norman for that matter—am no more special than you are. We are all special to God. We are perfect in his sight. God gave us a perfect body for our spirit and soul to live in. God does not make mistakes. You are exactly who God miraculously designed you to be.

With this in mind, why do most people desire a better body? Why aren't we satisfied with who we are? We should be exuberantly happy with this perfect body that God made just for us. Every one of us is unique.

I remember as a youngster growing up how I wanted to be like Daniel Boone or Davy Crocket, to be living a life of exploring the new frontier. But, you see, that would be impossible because God waited nearly six thousand years to get the right egg and the right spermatozoa so that I could be born, and that didn't happen until 1939. That particular egg and spermatozoa were not available until then.

God does not make mistakes. If you had been born blind and you asked God to heal you and give you sight, you would be telling God that he had made a mistake. Now if you were born with sight and then lost your sight, it would be good to ask God to restore your sight. Do you see the difference?

As Jesus ministered for three years, he had a large following. He fed five thousand, at one time on the side of a mountain. Every where that Jesus went the crowds would follow. Why? For salvation? No. They followed him because of his teaching, but mostly for his miracles, healing especially.

Jesus once healed a blind man that was blind from birth. Why? Did God make a mistake? No, he was born blind as God intended, but Jesus gave him sight to show the people that he was the Son of God that he claimed to be and to bring glory to his father.

> And as Jesus passed by, he saw a man which was blind from his birth. And his disciples asked him, saying, Master, who did sin, this man, or his parents, that he was blind. Jesus answered, neither hath this man sinned, nor his parents; but that the works of God should be made manifest in him. (John 9:1–3)

As far as I know this is the only time that Jesus healed a person with what we call a birth defect. So what is my point? That we are made perfect to become that part of the body of Christ that God intends for us to be. When we become believers, we become a part of his body, of which he is the head. You understand that our body is made up of many parts; so also is the body of Christ. My nose has a different function than my hand, and my foot differs from my ear. Each part of the body has its own unique position and function. We become that unique part of Christ's body at conversion.

When someone asks me to pray for them, I am more than happy to do so. We are called to pray for one and other, to lift each other up in prayer. But usually I don't pray for something specific. Someone might ask me for instance, to pray that they would get the job that they are interviewing for tomorrow. Well I just can't do that because that may not be what God has planned for them. So I pray that that person will accept what happens tomorrow as the result of God's will, whether they get the job or not.

God has a plan for every one of us. We are led by the Spirit of God to follow that plan when we become his child and not the child of Satan. We are a part of the body of Christ; where we fit into that body, we do not know, but God knows. He is the one that designed every part. We often try to be somebody that we were not meant to be and wonder why things don't work out so well for us. If you are a part of the hand, stop trying to breathe. Do you get my point? Stop trying to be someone or something that God did not design you to be.

If you are a prayer warrior, be a good one. Put all of your talents to work as you pray for others. Being a soul winner may not work for you; that may be a designated feature for another part of the body. So stop trying to do something that God did not design you to do; just pray for the other parts of the body to support them.

The local church is a good example of the body of Christ. You may be a piano player, a music director, a choir member, a sound technician, an usher, a greeter, a deacon, a teacher, or a preacher. They all have a different function, yet they all make up the body of the church.

The Wide and Narrow Gates

What percentage rate of all peoples of the earth today do you think will go to heaven? 100%? 1%? Or maybe somewhere in between? Let's take a look at what the Bible says on this subject.

> Enter ye in at the strait gate; for wide is the gate and broad is the way, that leadeth to destruction, and many there be which go in thereat. Because strait is the gate, and narrow is the way, which leadeth unto life, and few there be that find it. (Matt. 7:13–14)

Let's define many as 80% or more and few as 20% or less. I think that would be a fair understanding. So we can say by these scriptures that less than 20% will go to heaven. The flood (Noah's Ark), was 1,500 years after Adam and Eve were created. How many people would have been alive when the flood occurred? 1,500 years divided by 45 years (average for a generation), and we have 33 generations from Adam to Noah. There must have been many millions of people at that time, yet only eight people were saved. That would be far less than one-tenth of one percent.

You may find this hard to believe, so I want you to do this exercise for yourself. If you have never done this, you will be amazed. A calculator would be helpful but not necessary. If you came to work for me and I paid you one penny for the first day, and I doubled your wages every day for thirty days, I would be paying you more than one million dollars on the thirtieth day. Is this hard to believe? Do the exercise.

> [Elijah speaking] And I, even I only, am left, and they seek my life, to take it away. (1 Kings 19:14b)

> [God speaking] Yet I have left me seven thousand in Israel, all the knees which have not bowed unto Baal, and every mouth which hath not kissed him. (1 Kings 19:18)

Now seven thousand seems to be a lot of people, but that is only one-tenth of one percent of the estimated seven million Jews in Israel.

There are many scriptures where it is said that there was only a remnant left. A remnant would be a few—a very few. Here are some scriptures for you to take a look at: 2 Kings 19:30–31, 25:11; Isaiah 1:9, 16:14; Ezekiel 6:8; Romans 9:27, 11:5. There are many more scriptures on this subject.

As I read the Bible, I come to the conclusion that very few will be saved—less than one percent. In America there will be a larger percentage if the Lord comes back soon. Right now as a Christian nation we are failing God and getting worse. In the United States, 86% of the people claim to be Christians. Most likely because we are a Christian nation as opposed to Jewish, Muslim, Hindu, or any other religion. Of that 86% less than 50% attend church more than twice a year. About 20% to 25% of the three hundred million people attend church with some regularity. How many of these churches do not preach a salvation message or offer an altar call? There are whole denominations that do not.

Of all the churches in America, there are only a few that preach and teach us how to go to heaven. That being that a person must take God at his word by faith, believing that Jesus is the Son of God, died on the cross, shed his blood to pay the penalty of our sins, was buried, and was resurrected on the third day to give us eternal life.

Statistics alone show us that the number of born-again Christians in the United States is less than 10%, maybe much less, and we are a Christian nation. Some nations don't have any or very few Christians. So the answer to my original question on this subject, what percentage rate of all people on earth today do you think will go to heaven? I would have to say a very small remnant of less than one percent.

Hell, Sheol, and Hades

There is a lot of confusion here for a lot of people. Hell, Sheol, and Hades are one in the same place. It is the place for departed souls. The Old Testament was written in Hebrew. The place that we call hell today was a Hebrew word *Sheol*. The New Testament was written in Greek, and the Greek word is *Hades*. The word *Sheol* is not used in the Bible, and I think that is what confuses people when others use the word *Sheol* instead of *hell*. So it really boils down to two words: *hell* and *Hades*.

Hell and Hades are used interchangeably, and that is because they are referring to the same place. From here on we will refer to it as hell. Hell is divided in two parts; one side is referred to as paradise, and the other is known as hell, separated by what the Bible calls a great gulf. The hell side is the abode of the lost, and the paradise side was the abode of the departed saints. After Jesus died on the cross, he descended into hell to set the captive souls free from the paradise side of hell. I'm sure that this is as clear as mud. Paradise was also called Abraham's bosom.

Read Luke 16:19–31, which talks about the rich man and Lazarus. This is a good description of hell. Some think that this is one of Jesus's parables, but I think it is a factual account of two people. In none of Jesus's parables does he name names. Here he talks about the beggar Lazarus, but notice that he does not call the rich man by name. Possibly out of respect for the man's family. We don't want to hear that one of our loved ones went to hell; we always hang on to hope that they went to heaven.

When you die, if you are a child of God, your soul will go to paradise, and if you were a child of Satan, your soul will go to hell. That was before Christ died and was resurrected. Now for a child of God to die, his soul will go directly to heaven because when Christ died, he went to hell (paradise side) to take those souls to heaven. Hell is still the abode of the lost and has been since the beginning. But paradise is now empty.

Hell is like the local or county jail. If you are accused of a crime, you go to jail and stay there until your trial before a court room judge. If after the trial you have been found guilty, you are sent to prison, sometimes without the possibility of parole.

All those in hell (the jail) will be confronted by Jesus (the judge) at the great white throne judgment seat of Christ after his one-thousand-year reign. They will all be found guilty of sin and will be cast into the lake of fire (the prison). Their sentence will never end. It will be for eternity without the possibility of parole.

Many people think that their eternal home will be in heaven or hell. But this is not so. If when you dic and you go to hell, you will only be there until judgment day, then you will be cast into the lake of fire. If when you die, you go to heaven, you will only be there until God creates a new heaven and a new earth, where you will spend eternity with Christ on the new earth. This you will learn from the book of Revelation.

The True Church

I touched on this earlier, but I want to revisit this topic: the church. What I am writing here might upset a lot of teaching that you have gotten through the years. I hope that I can explain this in such a way that you might understand. If not, please research this for yourself. Hopefully you will be able to understand the difference between the church in Jerusalem and the true church, the body of Christ.

Christ ascended into heaven after forty days with his disciples after his resurrection. Ten days later the twelve apostles received the Comforter (the Holy Spirit), that Jesus had promised to send to them. This is called the day of Pentecost. This is found in Acts 2.

> Then they that gladly received his word were baptized; and the same day were added unto them about three thousand souls. (Acts 2:41)

> Praising God, and having favor with all the people, and the Lord added to the church daily, such as should be saved. (Acts 2:47)

What did this church believe? Did they believe and put their faith in the fact that Jesus died to pay for their sins? No. In Matthew 16 Christ said that he would build his church upon this rock. What is this rock that he was talking about?

> And I say also unto thee, That thou art Peter, and upon this rock I will build my church, and

> the gates of hell shall not prevail against it. (Matt. 16:18)

This church (ecclesia) is not to be built on Peter but on what Peter said in verse 16: "And Simon Peter said, Thou art the Christ, the Son of the Living God." This is what the Jews under the law were to believe. On the day of Pentecost, those that took part were Jews under the law. Acts 8:1 in part says, "And at that time there was great persecution against the church which was in Jerusalem." The persecution was mainly caused by Saul (Paul). In Acts 8:3 Saul makes havoc of the church. Why? Because the disciples were preaching that Jesus was the Son of God. This was counter to Saul's belief as a leader of the self-righteous lawkeeping Jews.

This church was a commune. They sold everything that they had and pooled their money together and shared equally with everyone. They were all equal. Today this would be called socialistic governing. And how did this work out? Well unfortunately, it didn't work well. It wasn't very long until the money ran out. Later in Acts, Paul was taking up offerings for the poor saints in Jerusalem. So what happened to this church in Jerusalem? I really don't have any idea what happened to this church. But I think that had they done what Jesus had instructed them to do in Acts 1:8, things would have been different.

> But ye shall receive power, after that the Holy Ghost is come upon you; and ye shall be witnesses unto me both in Jerusalem, and in

> Judea, and in Samaria, and unto the uttermost part of the earth. (Acts 1:8)

But they didn't go; they stayed in Jerusalem. About ten years later, Peter was shown a vision and went to the house of Cornelius, a Gentile. After this experience, Peter went right back to Jerusalem and stayed there with the rest of the disciples. And God then called on Saul.

All of this happened before God revealed the mystery of the true church (the body of Christ) to Paul. There is a vast difference between the church at Jerusalem and the seven churches that Paul started in Asia Minor. The church in Jerusalem believed that Jesus was the Son of God—and that's all, no death burial or resurrection—and that is all that they were expected to believe.

But God revealed to Paul the true church (the body of Christ). God's grace was revealed to Paul that faith in Christ's death, burial, and resurrection would be counted as our righteousness. The church in Jerusalem was ecclesiastical, meaning, "Pertaining to a church, especially as an organized institution. An organized body of people of like mind". The body of Christ is not an organization. It is a living organism, and Christ is the head of the body.

Faith plus Nothing

What is faith? Hebrews 11:1 says, "Now faith is the substance of things hoped for, the evidence of things not seen."

Hebrews 11 is called the faith chapter.

Verse 4: By faith Abel
Verse 5: By faith Enoch
Verse 7: By faith Noah
Verse 8: By faith Abraham
Verse 9: By faith sojourned
Verse 11: Through faith Sarah
Verse 13: These all died in faith

> But without faith it is impossible to please him: for he that cometh to God must believe that he is, and that he is a rewarder of them that diligently seek him. (Heb. 11:6)

We cannot come to God unless we have faith in him. It is impossible to please God without faith. Some people believe that to be saved you must join a church, or be baptized, or attend services on a regular basis, or tithe, or add on any number of things that they must do. That is called works. We do not have to do anything but believe and receive. We don't have to work for our salvation. Christ did all that was necessary for us to be saved. Our sin debt has been paid in full. So sin is not the issue anymore. The issue is whether or not you have faith believing that Jesus paid your sin debt.

> Therefore we conclude that a man is justified by faith without the deeds of the law. (Rom. 3:28)

In other words, we do not have to work for our salvation by following the law. It doesn't say that we are justified by faith and attending church or being baptized. So it is faith plus nothing.

> But to him that worketh not but believeth on him that justifieth the ungodly, his faith is counted for righteousness (Rom. 4:5).

> Knowing that a man is not justified by the works of the law, but by the faith of Jesus Christ, even we have believed in Jesus Christ, that we might be justified by the faith of Christ and not by the works of the law; for by the works of the law shall no flesh be justified (Gal. 2:16).

> Wherefore the law was our schoolmaster to bring us unto Christ, that we might be justified by faith [plus nothing] (Gal. 3:24).

> For ye are all children of God by faith [plus nothing] in Christ Jesus (Gal. 3:26).

> For by grace are you saved through faith; [plus nothing] and that not of yourselves, it is a gift of God: Not of works, lest any man should boast (Eph. 2:8–9).

> That Christ may dwell in your hearts by faith [plus nothing] that ye, being rooted and grounded in love (Eph. 3:17).

Are you getting the picture here? We are saved by our faith only; we do not have to join the church, or be baptized, or do anything except believe and receive.

> But wilt thou know, O, vain man, that faith without works is dead. (James 2:20)

At first glance this verse might sound like a contradiction, but it is saying that after you get saved by your faith, you do all these other things because of your salvation. We all have faith. We have faith that the alarm will go off at the right time, faith that the chair will hold us, faith that our car will start, and faith that the ice maker will be working when we need ice cubes.

But you have to exercise your faith by doing something. You can have all the faith in the world that your car will start, but if you don't put the key into the ignition, your faith is in vain. Remember the illustration of the man giving out the one-hundred-dollar bills? You do not get the benefit of the bill unless you take it. You do not get the benefit of your faith unless you exercise that faith. Faith without works is dead.

7

One Observation and Two Questions

I have an observation to share with you and two questions that I can't get a handle on at this time. The first question I will give an answer to by showing you what I mean about thinking outside of the box. The second question I have no answer for now, but God will shed light on this for me if he chooses. First, the observation. I don't recall hearing about it in this light:

In Matthew 22:1–14 a king was making a wedding feast for his son. He sent his servants to gather together those that were invited, but they did not come. He sent out other servants, but they still refused to come, making excuses. Then, when the servants pleaded with them to come, they killed the servants. The king then, after denouncing the unworthiness of the invited guests, sent out more servants and invited everyone, both good and bad, and they came, and the wedding feast was accomplished.

This is precisely what happened between God and the Jews. They rejected Christ and paved the way for the church. First, notice that this was a king, not a person of the general populace. The wedding feast was for his son. The first invited guests (the Jews) refused his invitation and killed the servants, and then the invitation went out to all that would come.

The king is God; the son, of course, is Jesus. God invited the Jews, but they refused and killed the servants (the prophets). God called the Jews unworthy and sent out more servants (Paul and Barnabas) to extend the invitation to all that would come. And this is where we are today, and the guests are still coming. Jesus has invited you to the wedding as his bride; will you refuse him as his firsts guests, the Jews did, or will you join me and become a part of his body, the bride? The Jews were invited to be guests; we are invited to be his bride. What a difference.

First question: Can you reconcile the difference between John 19:38–42 and the account of Luke 23:50–24:1? In John 19 Joseph of Arimathaea took the body of Jesus from the cross and, along with Nicodemus, brought a mixture of myrrh and aloes—about one hundred pounds. They wound the body of Jesus in linen clothes along with the spices, as required for a burial according to the Jewish custom. They placed his body in an unused sepulcher. Now contrast this with Luke 23.

He took Jesus from the cross and wrapped his body in linen and laid him in a sepulcher. The women also saw where and how Jesus was laid in the sepulcher and returned home to prepare spices and ointments for his body, but because the Sabbath was about to begin, they would have to wait until after the Sabbath.

Some things in scripture are hard to reconcile or understand. So which of these two are correct? John says that the two men prepared his body for burial, but Luke said that the women were going to the tomb on Sunday morning to prepare his body.

Now obviously one of these are wrong—or are they? Is it possible that both accounts are correct? Yes, but this is conjecture on my part, thinking outside of the box so to speak. In John, the two men wrapped the body of Jesus in spices and linen, and the women in Luke saw the two men laying Jesus's body in the tomb, but they did not realize that his body had already been prepared for burial. They made plans to prepare his body, but there was not time to do so before the Sabbath day.

Now the second question. Revelation 21:14 says "And the wall of the city had twelve foundations, and in them the names of the twelve apostles of the Lamb."

Can you name the twelve apostles? I can't; I'm not sure anyone can.

Matthew and Mark	Luke	John	Acts
Peter	Peter	Andrew	Peter
Andrew	Andrew	Peter	James
James	James	Phillip	John
John	John	Nathanael	Andrew
Phillip	Philip	Judas	Phillip
Bartholomew	Bartholomew	Thomas	Thomas
Thomas	Matthew	John	Bartholomew
Matthew	Thomas	Judas	Matthew
James	James	James	James
Thaddaeus	Simon	Simon	
Simon	Judas	Judas	
Judas	Judas	Matthias	

Matthew and Mark agree; the others do not. I have heard that sometimes their nicknames were used. But that doesn't sound like a good explanation to me. Who will have their name in the twelve foundations of the new city of Jerusalem? I believe that one of them will be Matthias, the one that replaced Judas, but I'm not too sure on that either.

Eternity or Eternal?

Deuteronomy 33:27 says "The eternal God is thy refuge." God is eternal, but what does eternal mean? As described in the dictionary: "Without beginning or end; existing outside of time." Are you and I eternal? Yes, we are. Our body is not, but our soul and spirit are.

Even though we will all die, we will all live forever—some into eternal life, and some into eternal death. In either case, we shall all, both spirit and soul, live forever.

> And these shall go away into everlasting punishment; but the righteous into life eternal. (Matt. 25:46)

Eternal Life	**Eternal Death**
Matthew 19:16	Mark 3:29
John 10:28	Hebrews 6:2
Mark 10:30	Jude 7
John 17:2	
Luke 10:25	
Romans 5:21	
John 3:15	
Romans 6:23	

All of these scriptures verify that we are eternal. We have a choice of where we will spend the rest of eternity. In the dictionary, there are two different definitions of eternity. Number one is that there is no beginning and no ending (having always been and always will be). Number two is as having a beginning but no ending (such as an eternal flame). So which are we? According to Deuteronomy 33:27 God has always been and always will be. But what about us? Did we become eternal when we were born, or do we become eternal when we die, or have we been with God in spirit and soul from the beginning?

All of the scriptures about eternal or eternity have to do with life after our birth or death—that is, our physical being. But what about our soul and spirit before our physical birth? Did God know us then? I believe that he did.

> Before I formed thee in the belly, I knew thee; and before thou camest forth out of the womb, I sanctified thee, and I ordained thee a prophet unto the nations. (Jer. 1:5)

God knew Jeremiah before his mother conceived him in her womb. God did not say "I knew of you." He said, "I knew you [past tense]."

For some, this might be a real stretch. Think outside of the box and go with me on this; you might at least think it interesting. I am a member of the body of Christ, and Christ is the head of the body.

> Let us be glad and rejoice, and give honor to him: for the marriage of the Lamb is come, and his wife hath made herself ready. And to her was granted that she should be arrayed in fine linen, clean and white: for the fine linen is the righteousness of the saints. And he saith unto me, write Blessed are they which are called unto the marriage supper of the Lamb. And he said unto me, These are the true sayings of God. (Rev. 19:7–9)

The Lamb is Christ, and we, the true church, are to be his wife. Christ is the head of the church and we, the church, are his body. We will be united in marriage to Jesus the Christ when the body is complete. In verse 7 it says that the wife has made herself ready. That is to say that the last part of the body of Christ has come to join the rest of the body to make it complete.

> And Adam said, this is now bone of my bones, and flesh of my flesh: she shall be called woman, because she was taken out of man. Therefore shall a man leave his father and his mother and shall cleave unto his wife: and they shall be one flesh. (Gen. 2:23–24)

At marriage, a man and his wife become one flesh. When Christ is married to the church, we will become one flesh. We will become one with Christ. Christ is God. We will become one with God.

I believe that is where our soul and spirit where in the beginning—with God. We will be right back where we started from, but now we will have a glorified body that will live forever.

All souls come from God, good or bad. All arc subject to God. God wanted those souls to have a choice on whether or not they choose to love him. That is why he made Adam and Eve. We all have to make a choice. We are all born in sin, and unless we choose to love and obey God, we will all die in our sins and live outside of God's presence.

In Revelation 20:11–15 we read of the great white throne of God. This is where God passes judgment on the nonbeliever. The outcome is in verses 14 and 15:

> And death and hell were cast into the lake of fire. This is the second death. And whosoever was not found written in the book of life was cast into the lake of fire. (Rev. 20:14–15)

How about you? Is your name written in the Lamb's book of life? It is recorded in the book of life when you accept by faith the finished work of the cross.

We do not become sinners because we have sinned, but we sin because we are sinners. Read this again so that you understand what you just read. We are born in sin; we don't become sinners.

Every man, woman, and child are born sinners, and we all deserve God's judgment. But because of his grace, he pardons us from punishment if we choose to accept him at his word. Remember in the beginning of this book how I told you about the importance of the word *if*? Here you can see that the word *if* is a matter of choice.

Omnipresent

The definition of *omnipresent* is "The faculty or power of being present in every place all of the time, an attribute particular to God." According to the *American Heritage Dictionary*, God is everywhere at the same time—always. God is also said to be omnipotent—all powerful—and omniscience—having all knowledge.

In Revelation 19:6 it says "For the Lord God omnipotent reigneth." I think that this is the only time that one of these three omni words is used in the Bible.

I understand and accept the idea of an all-powerful and all-knowing God, but I don't understand how he is said to be everywhere at all times. I can accept that God can be anywhere when he chooses to be there.

> Whither shall I go from thy spirit? Or whither shall I flee from thy presents? If I ascend up into heaven, thou art there; If I make my bed in hell, behold, thou art there. (Ps. 139:7–8)

I think what David is saying is that he cannot go anywhere where God can't find him. God can be where he wants to be when he wants to be there. It is said that hell is eternal separation from God. To spend eternity without God implies that he is not there. Is God in the heart of a nonbeliever? I don't think so. Then to me, God is not omnipresent as the word is described in the dictionary.

Can you name the three angels mentioned in the Bible? This could be a trick question depending on your belief. One is Gabriel (the messenger) mentioned in Daniel 8:16, 9:21 and again in Luke 1:19, 26. Another angel is Michael (mighty warrior) mentioned in Daniel 10:13, 10:21, and 12:1; Jude 9; and Revelation 12:7. You probably got these two correct, but what about the third angel that is named in scripture? Now some of you may disagree that this third one is actually an angel. His name is Lucifer. He is introduced in Isaiah 14:12–14.

How art thou fallen from heaven, O Lucifer, son of the morning! How art thou cut down to the ground, which did weaken the nations! For thou hast said in thine heart, I will ascend into heaven; I will exalt my throne above the stars of God: I will sit also upon the mount of the congregation, in the sides of the north. I will ascend above the heights of the clouds, I will be like the most High.

Son of man, take up a lamentation upon the king of Tyrus, and say unto him, Thus saith the Lord God; Thou sealest up the sum, full of wisdom, and perfect in beauty. Thou hast been in Eden the garden of God; every precious stone was thy covering, the sardius, topaz, and the diamond, the beryl, the onyx, and the jasper, the sapphire, the emerald, and the carbuncle, and gold; the workmanship of thy tabrets and of thy pipes was prepared in thee in the day that thou wast created. Thou art the anointed cherub that covereth; and I have set thee so; thou wast upon the holy mountain of God; thou hast walked up and down in the midst of the stones of fire. Thou was perfect in thy ways from the day that thou was created, till iniquity was found in thee. By the multitude of thy merchandise they have filled the midst of thee with violence, and thou hast sinned: therefore I will cast thee as profane out of the mountain of God: and I will destroy thee, O covering cherub, from the midst of the stones of fire. Thine heart was lifted up because of thy beauty,

> thou hast corrupted thy wisdom by reason of thy brightness: I will cast thee to the ground, I will lay thee before kings, that they may behold thee. (Ezek. 28:12–17)

In my mind there is no doubt that Isaiah and Ezekiel are describing the same angelic being that rebels against God. An angelic being is in Ezekiel 28:14: the anointed cherub. A cherub is an angel. In verse 12 he is called the king of Tyrus. This is an allegory.

If you were to put on a play or a skit about Adam and Eve in the garden of eden, who would be on the list of characters? Let's see: First, you would have God, and there is Adam and Eve, and it seems that I am missing someone else. Oh, yes, the serpent; now my actors are in place.

Now read Ezekiel 28:13 again: "Thou hast been in the garden of Eden, the garden of God." This is not God; it is not Adam or Eve, so it must be the serpent. This king of Tyrus cannot be a person; the garden of eden experience happened 3,400 years before Ezekiel wrote these scriptures.

I believe that the serpent in the garden was the incarnate body of Satan; I covered this in chapter 2. Satan used the serpent because evidently Eve had had conversations with the serpent before because she didn't seem to be startled by the serpent speaking to her. Now let me give you one more scripture concerning the serpent.

And the great dragon was cast out, that old serpent, called the Devil, and Satan, which deceived the whole world: he was cast out into the earth, and his angels were cast out with him. (Rev. 12:9)

8

The Book of Revelation

Revelation reveals the future of the Jews, the Gentiles, the church, and Jesus Christ as the King of kings and the Lord of lords. The book contains details of the Savior's return, the establishment of his millennial kingdom, and the eternal destiny of the lost and the saved. Revelation is a Greek word *apakolupsis* meaning "unveiling or uncovered." From this we get the word *apocalypse*.

Tribulation describes a period of seven years of turmoil for Jews and Gentiles that coincide with Daniel's seventieth week. A peace treaty is signed with Israel for seven years, and it is broken after forty-two months by Satan's reincarnation of the beast (Antichrist), forcing people to receive the mark of the beast. It is also described as being called a time of Jacob's trouble. (Jacob is Israel.)

Rapture is derived from the Latin words *rapio*, *rapere*, or *raptus*, meaning "a snatching away."

Church is the body of Christ in which Christ is the head of the body of believers (the body of Christ).

The millennium is a thousand-year period where Christ rules and Satan is bound in the bottomless pit.

The satanic trinity are the dragon (anti-God), the beast (Antichrist), and the false prophet [anti-Spirit]. Satan has a counterfeit for everything that God has.

In chapter 6 that is not Christ on the white horse. That is Satan or one of his angels. Christ returns to earth on a white horse in chapter 19.

> Write the things which thou hast seen, and the things which are, and the things which shall be hereafter. (Rev. 1:19)

In this scripture, time is divided as past, present, and future. The past, of course, is anything prior to John's vision on the Isle of Patmos. Chapters 1, 2, and 3 pertain to the things that are. Chapters 4 through 22 pertain to the things that shall be.

> After this I looked, and behold, a door was opened in heaven: and the first voice which I heard was as it were of a trumpet talking with me; which said, Come up hither, And I will shew thee things which must be hereafter. (Rev. 4:1)

After what? After the things concerning the seven churches in Asia. This is when, I believe, that the church is raptured into heaven. John hears a voice that sounds like a trumpet. 1 Corinthians 15:51–53 and 1 Thessalonians 4:13–17 are two of the places that describe the rapture of the church.

> In a moment, in the twinkling of an eye, at the last trump. (1 Cor. 15:52)
>
> For the Lord himself shall descend from heaven with a shout, with the voice of the archangel, and with the trump of God. (1 Thess. 4:16)

The church is not mentioned again until the Lord returns as King of kings and Lord of lords in chapter 19 in regards to the church on earth. From chapter 4 until chapter 19 the church is in heaven at the wedding feast of the Lamb (Christ). We will be receiving rewards; a crown of righteousness will be given to all those who received God's salvation, and other crowns will be given for other services.

So the things that shall be, starting in chapter 4 through 18, do not involve the church. This is a time set aside that Israel must go through before Christ can set up his kingdom here on earth.

Do you remember that I wrote earlier that every promise that God made to Abraham and the Jewish nation throughout the Bible are all earthly promises? There are no promises to Israel as a nation in the heavenly realm. All promises are earthly. This can't be stated enough.

On the other hand, all promises to the church are heavenly. God does not promise us earthly wealth and prosperity as he did the Jews. All of the Jewish rewards are earthly, and all of the rewards of the saints will be given out in heaven. I hope that you get this; it is so important for you to understand this. Don't mix the church with the nation of Israel.

Chapters 1, 2, and 3 The seven churches

4:1	The rapture of the church
6:1	Opening of the seals
8:7	Sounding of the trumpets
16:1	Pouring out of the vials
19:7	Marriage of the Lamb
19:11	Christ's return
19:20	Beast and False Prophet, Lake of Fire
20:1	Satan cast into bottomless pit
20:7	Satan loosed for a little season
20:10	Satan cast into Lake of Fire
20:12	Sinners follow after Satan
21:1	New heaven and new earth
21:2	New city of Jerusalem
21:9	Description of new city
22:12	God's warning to be prepared
22:18	Do not add to or take away from this book

If you have received Christ as your savior, all of these terrible events that happen here on earth from chapter 4 through 18 should not concern you, so don't get all worked up because you can't understand the symbolisms described. On the other hand, you may want to show some concern if you are on the outside looking in.

Basically, John used these symbolisms for one of two different reasons. That is what God showed him, or what he saw he could not describe, such as an airplane, atomic weapons, or a tank. The beasts are the same or similar to Daniel's beast, and the plagues are like what God put upon Egypt in Exodus. The plagues speak for themselves, and the beasts represent nations.

To me, the book of Revelation confirms in me the fact that there is great conflict between good and evil and by God's grace shown unto me that I am a member of the winning team. I know the outcome of this conflict. and God wins. And because God wins, I win.

SECTION II

Thus far we have skimmed through the Bible and covered many topics.

In this section you will read about:

Jesus's teaching on prayer

Why he came to earth

What he preached

Before the cross—many

After the cross—all

The two churches

Earthly verses heavenly

The two resurrections—the righteous and the unrighteous

Timelines depicting the church age and what will follow into eternity

9

PRAYER

What is prayer?

1. A reverent petition made to a deity or other object of worship.
2. The act of making such a petition.
3. Any act of communion with God, such as confession, praise or thanksgiving.
4. A specially worded form used in addressing God.
5. A religious service in which praying predominates
6. Any fervent request.

Jesus's Instructions on Prayer

The scriptures below are my shortened version to show a thought:

> Matthew 6:5–8: Don't pray in public looking to exalt yourself. Go to your private place and meet with God on a personal basis.

5:44: Pray for those that do you wrong.

6:31–33: Don't worry about your earthly needs, seek ye first the kingdom of God, and his righteousness and all these things will be yours

7:7: Ask, and it shall be given you; seek, and you will find; knock, and it shall be opened unto you;

18:19–20: If two of you agree on anything, ask the heavenly father and he will give it to you, because where two or three are gathered together in my name, there am I in the midst.

21:21–22: Jesus said, if you have faith, and doubt not, whatever you ask for you will receive. Ask in prayer believing and you will receive.

Mark 11:24: Whatever you desire, in prayer, believe that you will receive it and you will.

11:25–26: Forgive others so that God will forgive you. If you do not, God will not forgive you.

John 15:7: If ye abide [endure patiently] in me and my words abide in you, ask anything and it will be done.

15:16: You did not choose me, but I chose you, so ask of the father anything in my name and he will give it to you.

When I first started reading the Bible, I would wonder why I didn't get what I prayed for. I asked God in Jesus's name, I had faith, I believed, yet I did not get what I prayed for. I did what Jesus said to do yet was without results.

So I asked other Christians, even my pastor. Their answer was basically the same. Either I lacked faith or I was praying for something outside of God's will for me.

Well I thought that my faith was good enough—strong enough. After all, I had read that if I had the faith of a mustard seed, I could say to that mountain, "Be cast into the sea," and it would be done. So it doesn't take a huge amount of faith—just a little bit would be enough—so as far as I was concerned, faith was not the issue; it must be God's will.

Well I read these verses again and it doesn't say anything about his will. Now I was really confused. Jesus said that if I asked the Father in Jesus's name that God the Father would give it to me.

There are basically two reasons that I started studying the Bible, and that was the first. Now the second thing that I had asked myself is when a rich man came to Jesus asking him, "What must I do to be saved?"

I was expecting Jesus to say something like, "When you feel the Holy Spirit tugging at your heartstrings, go forward in the church and receive Jesus as your Savior." But that is not what he told him. Jesus said that he must keep the law of Moses and sell everything that he had and to give the money to the poor.

I studied for years and was just confused until I learned to rightly divide the word of God.

What Jesus taught under the law and what Paul taught under grace. The following verses are all or most all of the verses in the New Testament containing the words *pray*, *prayer*, *praying*, *prayed*, and *prayest.* First the Jewish books under law, then Paul's epistles.

Praying Under the Law

> And when thou prayest, thou shalt not be as the hypocrites are: for they love to pray standing in the synagogues and in the corners of the streets, that they may be seen of men. Verily I say unto you, They have their reward. But thou, when thou prayest, enter into thy closet, and when thou hast shut thy door, pray to the Father which is in secret; and thy Father which seeth in secret shall reward thee openly. But when ye pray, use not vain repetitions, as the heathen do: for they think that they shall be heard for their much speaking. Be not ye therefore like unto them: for your Father knoweth what things ye have need of, before ye ask him. After this manner therefor pray ye; Our Father which art in heaven, Hallowed be thy name. Thy kingdom come. Thy will be done in earth, as it is in heaven. Give us this day our daily bread. And forgive us our debts, as we forgive our debtors. And lead us not into temptation, but deliver us from evil:

For thine is the kingdom, and the power, and the glory, forever. Amen. (Matt. 6:5–13)

Therefore take no thought, saying, What shall we eat? or, What shall we drink? or, Wherewithal shall we be clothed? (For after all these things do the Gentiles seek:) for your heavenly Father knoweth that ye have need of all these things. But seek ye first the kingdom of God, and his righteousness; and all these things shall be added unto you. (Matt. 6:31–33)

Ask and it shall be given you; seek, and ye shall find; knock and it shall be opened unto you; For every one that asketh receiveth; and he that seeketh findeth; and to him that knocketh it shall be opened. (Matt. 7:7–8)

Again I say unto you, That if two of you shall agree on earth as touching anything that they shall ask, it shall be done for them of my Father which is in heaven, For where two or three are gathered together in my name, there am I in the midst of them. (Matt. 18:19–20)

Jesus answered and said unto them, Verily I say unto you, If ye have faith, and doubt not, ye shall not only do this which is done to the fig tree, but also if ye shall say unto this mountain, Be thou removed, and be thou cast into the sea; it shall be done. And all things, whatsoever ye shall ask in prayer, believing, ye shall receive. (Matt. 21:21–22)

And he said unto them, This kind can come forth by nothing, but by prayer and fasting. (Mark 9:29)

And Jesus answering saith unto them, Have faith in God. For verily I say unto you, That whosoever shall say unto this mountain, Be thou removed, and be thou cast into the sea; and shall not doubt in his heart, but shall believe that those things which he saith shall come to pass; He shall have whatsoever he saith. Therefore I say unto you, What things so ever ye desire, when ye pray, believe that ye receive them, and ye shall have them. And when ye stand praying, forgive, if ye have ought against any: that your Father also which is in heaven may forgive you your trespasses. But if ye do not forgive, neither will your Father which is in heaven forgive your trespasses. (Mark 11:22–26)

And it came to pass in those days, that he went out into a mountain to pray, and continued all night in prayer to God. (Luke 6:12)

And it came to pass about an eight days after these sayings, he took Peter and John and James, and went up into a mountain to pray. And as he prayed, the fashion of his countenance was altered, and his raiment was white and glistering. (Luke 9:28–29)

If ye abide in me, and my words abide in you, ye shall ask what ye will, and it shall be done unto you. (John 15:7)

Ye have not chosen me, but I have chosen you, and ordained you, that ye should go and bring forth fruit, and that your fruit should remain: that whatsoever ye shall ask of the Father in my name, he may give it you. (John 15:16)

And in that day ye shall ask me nothing. Verily, verily, I say unto you, Whatsoever ye shall ask the Father in my name, he will give it you. Hitherto have ye asked nothing in my name; ask, and ye shall receive, that your joy may be full. (John 16:23–24)

And whatsoever ye shall ask in my name, that will I do, that the Father may be glorified in the Son. If ye ask anything in my name I will do it. (John 14:13–14)

These all continued with one accord in prayer and supplication, with the women, and Mary the mother of Jesus, and with his brethren. (Acts 1:14)

And they prayed, and said, Thou, Lord, which knowest the hearts of all men, shew whether of these two thou hast chosen. (Acts 1:24)

And they continued steadfastly in the apostles' doctrine and fellowship, and in breaking of bread, and in prayers. (Acts 2:42)

And when they had prayed, the place was shaken where they were assembled together; and they were all filled with the Holy Ghost, and they spake the word of God with boldness. (Acts 4:31)

Whom they set before the Apostles: and when they had prayed, they laid their hands on them. (Acts 6:6)

Who, when they were come down, prayed for them, that they might receive the Holy Ghost. (Acts 8:15)

Repent therefore of this thy wickedness, and pray God, if perhaps the thought of thine heart may be forgiven thee. (Acts 8:22)

Then answered Simon, and said, Pray ye to the Lord for me, that none of these things which ye have spoken come upon me. (Acts 8:24)

But Peter put them all forth, and kneeled down, and prayed; and turning him to the body said, Tabatha, arise. And she opened her eyes: and when she saw Peter, she sat up. (Acts 9:40)

A devout man, and one that feared God with all his house, which gave much alms to the people, and prayed to God always. (Acts 10:2)

On the morrow, as they went on their journey, and drew neigh unto the city, Peter went up upon the housetop to pray about the sixth hour. (Acts 10:9)

And Cornelius said, Four days ago I was fasting until this hour; and at the ninth hour I prayed in my house, and, behold, a man stood before me in bright clothing. (Acts 10:30)

If any of you lack wisdom, let him ask of God, that giveth to all men liberally, and upbraideth not; and it shall be given him. But let him ask in faith, nothing wavering. For he that wavereth is like a wave of the sea driven with the wind and tossed. For let not that man think that he shall receive anything of the Lord. (James 1:5–7)

Ye lust, and have not: ye kill, and desire to have, and cannot obtain: ye fight and war, yet ye have not, because ye ask not. Ye ask, and receive not, because ye ask amiss that ye may consume it upon your lusts. (James 4:2–3)

Is any among you afflicted? let him pray. Is any merry? let him sing psalms. Is any sick among you? let him call for the elders of the church; and let them pray over him, anointing him with oil in the name of the Lord: And the prayer of faith shall save the sick, and the Lord shall raise him up; and if he have committed sins, they shall be forgiven him. Confess your faults one to another, and pray one for another, that ye may be healed. The effectual fervent prayer of a righteous man availeth much. Elias was a man subject to like passions as we are, and he prayed earnestly that it might not rain; and it rained not on the earth by the space of three years and six months. And he prayed again, and the heaven gave rain, and the earth brought forth her fruit. (James 5:13–18)

Likewise, ye husbands, dwell with them according to knowledge, giving honor to the wife, as unto the weaker vessel, and as being heirs together of the grace of life; that your prayers be not hindered. (1 Pet. 3:7)

For the eyes of the Lord are over the righteous, and his ears are open unto their prayers; but the face of the Lord is against them that do evil. (1 Pet. 3:12)

But the end of all things is at hand: be ye therefore sober, and watch unto prayer. (1 Pet. 4:7)

And whatsoever we ask, we receive of him, because we keep his commandments, and do those things that are pleasing in his sight. (1 John 3:22)

These things have I written unto you that believe on the name of the Son of God; that ye may know that ye have eternal life, and that ye may believe on the name of the Son of God. And this is the confidence that we have in him, that if we ask any thing according to his will, he heareth us: And if we know that he hear us, whatsoever we ask, we know that we have the petitions that we desired of him. (1 John 5:13-15)

> But ye, beloved, building up yourselves on your most holy faith, praying in the Holy Ghost. (Jude 20)

Notice how often Jesus said ask anything and I will give it to you. Peter, James, and John also say the same thing—ask, and you will receive. Jesus is speaking to the Twelve, in particular, and to the leaders of the Jewish people in general, as well as the people themselves.

Praying Under Grace

> And at midnight Paul and Silas prayed, and sang praises unto God: and the prisoners heard them. (Acts 16:25)

> And when he had thus spoken, he kneeled down, and prayed with them all. (Acts 20:36)

> And when we had accomplished those days, we departed and went our way; and they all brought us on our way, with wives and children, till we were out of the city, and we kneeled down on the shore and prayed. (Acts 21:5)

> And it came to pass, that, when I was come again to Jerusalem, even while I prayed in the temple, I was in a trance. (Acts 22:17)

> And it came to pass, that the father of Publius lay sick of a fever and of a bloody flux: to whom Paul entered in, and prayed and laid his hands on him, and healed him. (Acts 28:8)

We give thanks to God always for you all, making mention of you in our prayers. (1 Thess. 1:2)

Night and day praying exceedingly that we might see your face, and might perfect that which is lacking in your faith. (1 Thess. 3:10)

Pray without ceasing. (1 Thess. 5:17)

And the very God of peace sanctify you wholly; and I pray God your whole spirit and soul and body be preserved blameless unto the coming of our Lord Jesus Christ. (1 Thess. 5:23)

Brethren, pray for us. (1 Thess. 5:25)

Defraud ye not one to the other, except it be with consent for a time, that ye may give yourselves to fasting and prayer; and come together again, that Satan tempt you not for your incontinency. (1 Cor. 7:5)

Every man praying or prophesying, having his head covered, dishonoureth his head. But every woman that prayeth or prophesieth with her head uncovered dishonoureth her head: for that is even all one as if she were shaven. (1 Cor. 11:4)

Wherefore let him that speaketh in an unknown tongue pray that he may interpret. For if I pray in an unknown tongue, my spirit prayeth, but my understanding is unfruitful. (1 Cor. 14:13–14)

Now then we are ambassadors for Christ, as though God did beseech you by us, we pray you in Christ's stead, be ye reconciled to God. (2 Cor. 5:20)

For God as my witness, whom I serve with my spirit in the gospel of his Son, that without ceasing I make mention of you always in my prayers. (Rom. 1:9)

Likewise the Spirit also helpeth our infirmities: for we know not what we should pray for as we ought: but the Spirit itself maketh intercession for us with groanings which cannot be uttered. And he that searcheth the hearts knoweth what is the mind of the Spirit, because he maketh intercession for the saints according to the will of God. (Rom. 8:26–27)

Brethren, my heart's desire and prayer to God for Israel is, that they might be saved. (Rom. 10:1)

Rejoicing in hope; patient in tribulation; continuing instant in prayer. (Rom. 12:12)

Now I beseech you, brethren, for the Lord Jesus Christ's sake, and for the love of the Spirit, that ye strive together with me in your prayers to God for me. (Rom. 15:30)

Now the God of peace be with you all. Amen. (Rom. 15:33)

We give thanks to God and the Father of our Lord Jesus Christ, praying always for you. (Col. 1:3)

Continue in prayer, and watch in the same with thanksgiving; Withal praying also for us, that God would open unto us a door of utterance, to speak the mystery of Christ, for which I am also in bonds. (Col. 4:2–3)

For this cause I bow my knees unto the Father of our Lord Jesus Christ. (Eph. 3:14)

Now unto him that is able to do exceeding abundantly above all that we ask or think, according to the power that worketh in us, Unto him be glory in the church by Christ Jesus throughout all ages, world without end. Amen. (Eph. 3:20–21)

Giving thanks always for all things unto God and the Father in the name of our Lord Jesus Christ. (Eph. 5:20)

Praying always with all prayer and supplication in the Spirit, and watching thereunto with all perseverance and supplication for all saints; And for me, that utterance may be given unto me, that I may open my mouth boldly, to make known the mystery of the gospel. (Eph. 6:18–19)

Always in every prayer of mine for you all making request with joy. (Phil 1:4)

> And this I pray, that your love may abound yet more and more in knowledge and in all judgement. (Phil. 1:9)
>
> For I know that this shall turn to my salvation through your prayer, and the supply of the Spirit of Jesus Christ. (Phil. 1:19)
>
> Be careful for nothing; but in everything by prayer and supplication with thanksgiving let your request be known unto God. (Phil. 4:6)
>
> I exhort therefore, that, first of all, supplications, prayers, intercessions, and giving of thanks, be made for all men. For kings, and for all that are in authority; that we may lead a quiet and peaceable life in all godliness and honesty. For this is good and acceptable in the sight of God our savior; Who will have all men to be saved, and to come unto the knowledge of the truth. (1 Tim. 2:1–4)
>
> I will therefore that men pray everywhere, lifting up holy hands, without wrath and doubting. (1 Tim. 2:8)

Did you notice the absence of "Ask anything in Christ's name and you will receive?" Do you see the difference between law and grace?

10

Why Did Jesus Come to Earth, And What Did He Preach?

Why Did Jesus Come to Earth?

> And she shall bring forth a son, and thou shalt call his name JESUS; for he shall save his people (The Jews) from their sins. (Matt. 1;21)

> And thou Bethlehem, in the land of Juda, art not the least among the princes of Juda: for out of thee shall come a governor, that shall rule my people Israel. (Matt. 2:6)

> But when the fullness of time was come, God sent forth his Son [Jesus] made of a woman [a Jew], made under the law. To redeem them that were under the law, [that is the Jews, not the church] that we, [the church] might receive the adoption of sons. (Gal. 4:4–5)

The above scriptures show that Jesus came to his people, the Jews. He did not come to call out a church for himself. That will come later after he would be rejected by his own people. Jesus came to fulfill the law and the prophets. The result of the Jews rejecting and killing Jesus paved the way for the Gentiles.

Jesus did not preach to nor have anything to do with Gentiles. He dealt strictly with the Jews under law; he did, however, deal with two Gentiles for healing.

We all have preconceived notions as to why Jesus came to earth. We got this from Sunday school or from preaching or just from our conversations with others. We were all, or mostly all, taught that Jesus came to die on the cross for our sins and that we could be saved from hell. Basically that is true, but Jesus came to his own, and his own received him not. Therefore, he called Paul to go to the Gentiles to call out a people for himself. The church (the body of Christ) did not come about until after the cross. Jesus' earthly ministry was to Jews only. His heavenly ministry is for Jew and Gentile. Thus the difference between law and grace.

The following scriptures are Jesus telling why he came:

> Think not that I am come to destroy the law, or the prophets: I am not come to destroy, but to fulfil. For verily I say unto you, Till heaven and earth pass, one jot or one tittle shall in no wise pass from the law, till all be fulfilled. (Matt. 5:17–18)

> But go ye and learn what that meaneth, I will have mercy, and not sacrifice: for I am not come

to call the righteous, but sinners to repentance. (Matt. 9:13)

These twelve Jesus sent forth, and commanded them, saying, go NOT into the way of the Gentiles, and into any city of the Samaritans enter ye not (I would venture to say that most people do not know that this verse is in their Bible.) But go rather to the lost sheep of the house of Israel. And as ye go, preach, saying, The kingdom of heaven is at hand. (Matt. 10:5–7)

But he answered and said, I am not sent but unto the lost sheep of the house of Israel. (Matt. 15:24)

For the Son of man is come to save that which was lost. (Matt. 18:11)

I came not to call the righteous, but sinners to repentance. (Luke 5:32)

I am come to send fire on the earth; and what will I, if it be already kindled? (Luke 12:49)

Suppose ye that I am come to give peace on earth? I tell you, nay; but rather division. (Luke 12:51)

For I came down from heaven, not to do mine own will, but the will of him that sent me. (John 6:38)

And Jesus said, For judgement I am come into this world, that they which see not might see;

> and that they which see might be made blind. (John 9:39)
>
> The thief cometh not, but for to steal, and to kill, and to destroy; I am come that they might have life, and that they might have it more abundantly. (John 10:10)
>
> Now is my soul troubled; and what shall I say? Father, save me from this hour: But for this cause came I unto this hour. (John 12:27)
>
> And if any man hear my words, and believe not, I judge him not: for I came not to judge the world, but to save the world. (John 12:47)
>
> Pilate therefore said unto him, Art thou a king then? Jesus answered, Thou sayest that I am a king. To this end was I born, and for this cause came I into the world, that I should bear witness unto the truth. Everyone that is of the truth heareth my voice. (John 18:37)

What Did Jesus Preach?

What Jesus preached goes hand-in-hand with why he came. Jesus preached the gospel of the kingdom to the Jews, that he was the Christ (Messiah), the king, and that the kingdom was at hand. He was the king that the Jews have been looking for, and if they would have accepted him as such, he could have ushered in the kingdom, but they rejected him and his offer.

From that time Jesus began to preach, and to say, Repent: for the kingdom of heaven is at hand. (Matt. 4:17)

And Jesus went about all Galilee, teaching in their synagogues, and preaching the gospel of the kingdom, and healing all manner of sickness and all manner of disease among the people. (Matt. 4:23)

And Jesus went about all the cities and villages, teaching in their synagogues, and preaching the gospel of the kingdom, and healing every sickness and every disease among the people. (Matt. 9:35)

And as you go, preach, saying, the kingdom of heaven is at hand. (Matt. 10:7)

Now after that John was put in prison, Jesus came unto Galilee, preaching the gospel of the kingdom of God. (Mark 1;14)

And he said unto them, I must preach the kingdom of God to other cities also: for therefore am I sent. (Luke 4:43)

Belief Under Law

Jew's Gospel

Now after that John was put in prison, Jesus came into Galilee, preaching the gospel of the kingdom of God. And saying, The time is fulfilled, and the kingdom of God is at hand:

repent ye, and believe the gospel [What gospel? The gospel of the kingdom.]. Mark 1:14–15)

Afterward he appeared unto the eleven as they sat at meat, and upbraided them with their unbelief and hardness of heart, because they believed not them which had seen him after he was risen.

And he said unto them, [the eleven disciples, not the true church, the body of Christ, as so many believe and preach] go ye into all the world, and preach the gospel to every creature [What gospel? Again the gospel of the kingdom. Paul's gospel to the Gentile churches did not come about until many years later.].

He that believeth and is baptized shall be saved, but he that believeth not shall be damned [Believe what? The death burial and resurrection? No, of course not, that had not happened yet. They were to believe the gospel of the kingdom. What God expected them to believe was the gospel of the kingdom and that Jesus was the Christ and that is all. Then they were to repent and be baptized.] And these signs shall follow them that believe: In my name they shall cast out devils; they shall speak with new tongues. They shall take up serpents; and if they drink any deadly thing, it shall not hurt them; they shall lay hands on the sick, and they shall recover. (Mark 16:14–18)

These last two scriptures do not depict the true church (Mark 16:17–18). I hope that you can see the difference between law and grace.

> He came unto his own, and his own received him not [the Jews]. But as many as received him, to them [the Jews], gave he power to become the sons of God. Even to them that believed [in the death, burial, and resurrection]. No, on his name: (John 1:11–12)

In John 6:29–59 (paraphrasing), Jesus is teaching that he was sent by God the Father to give eternal life to all that believe in him, that he is indeed who he said that he was, the son of the living God. This is the people of Israel that were fed the previous day on the hillside—the five thousand.

> And we believe and are sure that thou art that Christ, the Son of the living God. (John 6:69)

> But ye believed not, because ye are not of my sheep, as I said unto you. (John 10:26)

> He came unto his own, and his own received him not. (John 1:11)

> My sheep here my voice, and I know them, and they follow me. (John 10:27)

Nowhere in scripture is the church called *sheep*. This term is used only in reference to the people of Israel.

> And I gave unto them eternal life; and they shall never perish, neither shall any man pluck them out of my hand. (John 10:28)

> She saith unto him, yea, Lord: I believe that thou art the Christ, the Son of the living God, which should come into the world. (John 11:27)

> But these are written, that ye might believe that Jesus is the Christ, the Son of God, and that believing ye might have life through his name. (John 20:31)

> But when they believed Philip preaching the things concerning the kingdom of God, and the name of Jesus Christ, they were baptized, both men and women. (Acts 8:12)

> And Philip said, if thou believest with all thine heart, thou mayest. And he answered and said, I believe that Jesus Christ is the Son of God. (Acts 8:37)

All of these scriptures are about the Jews under the law. All that they were to believe is that Jesus is the Christ, the son of the living God. It has nothing to do with his death, burial, and resurrection.

11

Before and After the Cross

Christ Died For Many as Seen by the Jews under Law

Before Jesus died on the cross, he said that he came to die for *many*, not all.

> But when the fullness of the time was come, God sent forth his Son, made of a woman, made under the law. To redeem them that were under the law, that we might receive the adoption of sons. (Gal. 4:4–5)

> For the transgression of my people was he stricken. (Isa. 53:8b)

> By his knowledge shall my righteous servant justify many; for he shall bare their iniquities. Isa. 53:11b)

> And he bare the sins of many, and made intercession for the transgressors. (Isa. 53:12b)

> Even as the Son of man came not to be ministered unto, but to minister, and to give his life a ransom for many. (Matt. 20:28)

> For this is my blood of the new testament, which is shed for many for the remission of sins. (Matt. 26:28)

> So Christ was once offered to bare the sins of many; and unto them that look for him shall he appear the second time without sin unto salvation. (Heb. 9:28)

Before the cross, Jesus's commandment to the disciples was in Matthew 10:5. "These twelve Jesus sent forth and command them, saying, Go not into the way of the Gentiles and into any city of the Samaritans enter ye not."

Christ Died For All, as Seen by the Church (the Body of Christ)

After Jesus died, it is said that he died for *all.*

> For when we were yet without strength, in due time Christ died for the ungodly [All are by nature ungodly.]. (Rom. 5:6)

> But God commandeth his love toward us, in that, while we were yet sinners, Christ died for us. (Rom. 5:8)

> Wherefore, as by one man sin entered into the world, and death by sin; and so death passed upon all men, for that all have sinned. (Rom. 5:12)

> For the love of Christ constraineth us; because we thus judge, that if one died for all, then were all dead: And that he died for all, that they which live should not henceforth live unto themselves, but unto him which died for them, and rose again. (2 Cor. 5:14–15)

> By the which will we are sanctified through the offering of the body of Jesus Christ once for all. (Heb. 10:10)

After the cross, Jesus's commandment changed to:

> But ye shall receive power, after that the Holy Ghost is come upon you: and ye shall be witnesses unto me both in Jerusalem, and in all Judaea, and in Samaria, and unto the uttermost part of the earth. (Acts 1:8)

12

The Church Under Law Versus the True Church

Under Law

The church in Acts 2 began in Jerusalem. On the day of Pentecost there were Jews in Jerusalem from all over the known world that had been dispersed by the Babylonians in about 500 BC to celebrate the feast day. This church was for Jews only. It differs from Paul's churches in many ways.

The apostles were taught by Jesus to preach the gospel. Matthew 10:7, for example, says, "And as ye go, preach, saying, The kingdom of heaven is at hand." The Jews have been waiting for the Messiah to come to set up his kingdom. And what were these Jews to believe in order to enter into the kingdom? That Jesus is the Christ (Messiah). "Now when they heard this" (Acts 2:37). Who are they, and what did they hear? They were the thousands of Jews that had returned to Israel for the feast of Pentecost, and what they heard was that the works of Jesus and his resurrection prove that he was Christ.

Now go back to verse 37. "Now when they heard this, they were pricked in their heart, and said unto Peter and the rest of the apostles, Men and brethren, what shall we do?"

> Then Peter said unto them, Repent, and be baptized every one of you in the name of Jesus Christ for the remission of sins, and ye shall receive the gift of the Holy Ghost. (Acts 2:38)

> Then they that gladly received his word were baptized; and the same day there were added unto them about 3,000 souls. (Acts 2:41)

> He that believeth and is baptized shall be saved; but he that believeth not shall be damned. (Mark 16:16)

In Acts 2:38 Peter said, "Repent and be baptized then you will receive the Holy Spirit." These are all Jews. But when Peter went to the house of Cornelius, a law-keeping Gentile, they received the Holy Spirit and then were baptized. The Jews under the law were baptized and then received the Holy Spirit. The Gentiles under grace receive the Holy Spirit and then get baptized if they choose to get baptized. The Jews under law repent, get baptized, and then receive the Holy Spirit. The Gentiles under grace believe, receive the Holy Spirit, and then get baptized. I hope that you see the difference.

The church (*ecclesia*, meaning assembly) in Jerusalem were all in agreement that they would pool all of their resources together. Sell their lands and possessions and bring the money to the apostles. Then they would all share equally. This is in Acts 4:32–37. This was very serious because Ananias and Sapphira died at the feet of Peter because they kept part of their proceeds for themselves. These Jewish Christians were still under the law, and they were expecting Christ to return soon, to be their king in the soon-coming kingdom. They did not expect the money to run out. We call this a commune or a socialistic governance.

Jesus spent three years showing and proving that he in fact was the Christ that the scriptures had promised. Even after the cross he was still speaking of the things pertaining to the kingdom of God in Acts 1:3. And in verse 6, the apostles asked him, "Lord, will thou at this time restore again the kingdom to Israel?"

This church was to believe that Jesus was indeed the Christ. If they would turn away from their unbelief and believe that Jesus was the Christ, their sins would be forgiven, and they would be eligible to enter into the kingdom.

> But ye shall receive power after that the Holy Ghost is come upon you: and ye shall be witnesses unto me both in Jerusalem, and in all Judaea, and in Samaria and unto the uttermost part of the earth. (Acts 1:8)

This commission was given to the apostles, and they were to stay in Jerusalem until they received the Holy Spirit, which they did receive on the day of Pentecost. Then they were to go into *all* the world and preach the gospel of the kingdom. Compare this with Matthew 10:5–6. "These twelve Jesus sent forth, and commanded them, saying, GO NOT into the way of the Gentiles, and into any city of the Samaritans enter ye not. But go rather to the lost sheep of the house of Israel." But did they go as they were instructed in Acts 1:8? No, they did not. According to Acts 8:1, "And Saul was consenting unto his death. And at that time there was a great persecution against the church which was at Jerusalem; and they were all scattered abroad throughout the regions of Judaea and Samaria, *except the apostles* (emphasis mine)."

In fact, ten or fifteen years later they were still in Jerusalem when Paul and Barnabas went to Jerusalem to settle a dispute between Paul and the church in Jerusalem. This dispute was about circumcision and the keeping of the law. Read Acts 15:1–29 to get the full story.

> And when James, Cephas [Peter], and John, who seemed to be pillars, perceived the grace that was given unto me, they gave to me and Barnabas the right hands of fellowship; that we should go unto the heathen [Gentiles], and they unto the circumcision [Jews]. (Gal. 2:9)

I don't know what became of this church in Jerusalem. Did they eventually join up with Paul's church? Did they run out of funds? In some of Paul's epistles we find that Paul is taking offerings from the Gentile churches to the poor church in Jerusalem. Or did they become the Catholic Church and Peter was the first pope? Are there other possibilities?

The Church under Grace

According to Paul's Gospel

> And by him all that believe are justified from all things, from which ye could not be justified by the Law of Moses. (Acts 13:39)

> That the Gentiles by my mouth should hear the word of the gospel, and believe. (Acts 15:7)

Here Peter is retelling the episode of his preaching to Cornelius, a law-keeping Gentile. The gospel that Peter preached was the gospel under law, that being, that Jesus is the Christ, the son of the living God and that he would soon return to set up his kingdom. Paul's gospel of grace has not yet been revealed.

In fact, Paul said to the Philippian jailor in Acts 16:31, "And they said, Believe on the Lord Jesus Christ, and thou shalt be saved, and thy house."

At this point in time Paul had not received the mystery of the true church (the body of Christ), so nothing was mentioned about the death, burial, and resurrection. They had only to believe that Jesus was the

Christ. After Paul was shown the mystery of the true church, there arose a doctrinal difference between the church under Peter's leadership, which was still under law, and Paul's preaching to the Gentiles under grace.

The church under Peter's leadership were demanding that the Gentiles be circumcised to become proselytes of the Jews and to keep the law. A disagreement ensued, and Paul and Barnabas went to Jerusalem to settle this dispute. Peter stood up and related how that a long time ago how that he had gone to the house of Cornelius, presented the gospel, and God gave to them the Holy Spirit. You will find this in Acts 15.

> And when James, Cephas, and John, who seemed to be pillars, perceived the grace that was given to me, they gave to me and Barnabas the right hands of fellowship; that we should go unto the heathen [Gentiles], and they unto the circumcision [Jews]. (Gal. 2:9)

Paul's Turning Point

Those that believe that Jesus died to pay our sin debt and was buried and was resurrected on the third day are members of the church known as the body of Christ that Paul revealed as a mystery. And Christ is the head of the body (Eph. 1:22–23, 5:23; Col. 1:18).

Herein is Paul's gospel:

> Moreover, brethren, I declare unto you the gospel which I preached unto you, which also you have received, and wherein ye stand; By

> which also ye are saved, if ye keep in memory what I preached unto you, unless ye have believed in vain. For I delivered unto you first of all that which I also received, how that Christ died for our sins according to the scriptures; And that he was buried, and that he rose again the third day according to the scriptures (1 Cor. 15:1–4)
>
> For if we believe that Jesus died and rose again, even so them also which sleep in Jesus will God bring with him. (1 Thess. 4:14)
>
> Even the righteousness of God which is by faith of Jesus Christ unto all and upon all them that believe: for there is no difference. (Rom. 3:22)
>
> But the scripture hath concluded all under sin, that the promise by faith of Jesus Christ might be given to them that believe. (Gal. 3:22)

The faith *of* Jesus Christ is appropriated to us by our faith *in* Jesus Christ.

The Body of Christ

We that are born of the Spirit (I don't like to use the term *Christian* because it is used too loosely) are known as the body of Christ. What happened to Christ's body while here on earth? Jesus said that we would be mistreated, despised, hated, and be killed for his name's sake. It happened to him; it will happen to us.

Think about this for a second, Jesus did not die on the cross. Does this get your attention? His body died, but he did not. We do not die; only our body dies. We live on eternally, the saved and the lost. But we that are saved are the body of Christ. We will suffer along with Christ like he suffered. Here in America, not so much yet.

The only thing that God promised the church that is earthly is that we will be persecuted. But God promised us that through this persecution he would be with us. His grace is sufficient. I have to rely on God's word that his grace is all that I need in any situation. As we look around the world—or more pointedly, at the United States—through our politically correct society, we have taken God out of everything that we say or do.

It is hard for me to pray "God bless America." We have no right; in fact, it would be dead wrong to ask God to bless this nation that has turned our backs on him. He truly did bless this nation when we looked to him for guidance. Look back through America's history and how the founders (government) of this great nation believed God and sought his guidance and providence, and look at what we have become.

When I first read through the Bible, I would wonder, Why did Israel not learn from their mistakes? They would continually fall out of God's favor because of the sin of disobedience. They would repent after God punished them, God would forgive them, and bless them, and then in a very short time they again would disobey him. Is this not us? Are we any different? America will pay a high price for our unfaithfulness. We were on a slippery slope, but we have now gone over the cliff. The question now is, When we hit bottom—and we surely will—how hard will we hit?

While Christ was on earth, he endured extreme suffering. We are now his body; will we not suffer the same? Romans 6:6 says, “Knowing this, that our old man is crucified with him, that the body of sin might be destroyed, that henceforth we should not serve sin.” Romans 8:17 says, “And if children, then heirs; heirs of God, and joint-heirs with Christ; if so be that we suffer with him, that we may be also glorified together.” Philippians 1:29 says, “For unto you it is given in the behalf of Christ, not only to believe on him, but also to suffer for his sake.”

Earthly Versus Heavenly

In Genesis 13 God told Abram that his seed will be as the dust of the earth. In chapter 15 God told Abram that his seed would be as the stars in heaven. Why the difference?

> So also is the resurrection of the dead. It is sown in corruption; it is raised in incorruption: It is sewn in dishonor; it is raised in glory: it is sown in weakness; it is raised in power: It is sown a natural body; it is raised a spiritual body. There is a natural body, and there is a spiritual body. And so it is written, The first man Adam was

> made a living soul; the last Adam was made a quickening spirit. Howbeit that was not first which is spiritual, but that which is natural; and afterward that which is spiritual. The first man is of the earth, earthly; the second man is the Lord from heaven. (1 Cor. 15:42–47)

This format, earthly first then that which is heavenly, is used throughout the Bible. Some examples are Adam and Christ, Cain and Abel, Ishmael and Isaac, Esau and Jacob, and Saul and David, just to name a few. Every promise to Israel was earthly. If they kept God's commandments, they would receive a reward; the earthly kingdom that they were waiting for. God's first called-out people, Israel, were earthly. All promises to the church are heavenly. If we believe God's payment for our sins, we will receive crowns and rewards in heaven. The church is God's second called-out people—heavenly. I can't express this enough. Israel was never promised anything regarding heaven, and the church was never promised anything that is earthly.

At the time God called Abraham, the people of the earth were all Gentiles. As yet there were no Jews. In fact Abraham was never a Jew, nor was Isaac or Jacob. They are the fathers of the nation of Israel. But the nation of Israel was brought about in Egypt during the four hundred years of their captivity. Abraham believed God, and it was accounted to him for righteousness. Abraham had only to believe God; he did not have to do anything but believe. It is the same today for us. Les Feldick, a Bible teacher, calls this "faith plus nothing."

Abraham became the father of the nation of Israel. God called out a people from among the Gentiles for himself. To this people he would make himself known so that through them the whole world could know him. So first came the Gentiles (earthly), and then came Abraham, (heavenly), then came Israel (earthly). Israel rejected the son of God, and they killed him. Then God called out the church from among the Gentiles (heavenly). Christ said that the first would be last and the last shall be first.

This is all background information so that I can answer my original question concerning Genesis 13 and 15. What is the meaning of these scriptures? Genesis 13:16 says, "And I will make thy seed as the dust of the earth: so that if a man can number the dust of the earth, then shall thy seed also be numbered." This is the nation of Israel—earthly. Genesis 15:5 says, "And he brought him forth abroad, and said, Look now toward heaven, and tell the stars, if thou be able to number them: and he said unto him, So shall thy seed be." This is the church that will be grafted in—heavenly. I am amazed how all scripture fits together. How can anyone not believe that the Bible is the inspired word of God?

Abraham believed God, period—nothing added. Thus faith plus nothing. Did the prophets, priests, David, and other Jews believe faith plus nothing? Well no, they did not. They were required not only to believe but to sacrifice and to keep the law of Moses. So what is the difference? Abraham was a Gentile called by the grace of God because of his faith (heavenly). He was the forerunner of the church that would be called out by God's grace through faith plus nothing.

Did Jesus preach faith plus nothing? No. He preached repentance, believe, and be baptized. The same as Peter, James, and John, as well as John the Baptist. Paul preached Jesus Christ and him crucified. Where are you? With Peter, James, and John under law? Or Paul and the church under grace?

13

The Two Resurrections

The Righteous and the Unrighteous

Marvel not at this: for the hour is coming, in the which all that are in the graves shall hear his voice, And shall come forth; they that have done good, unto the resurrection of life; and they that have done evil, unto the resurrection of damnation. (John 5:28–29)

And have hope toward God, which they themselves also allow, that there shall be a resurrection of the dead, both of the just and unjust. (Acts 24:15)

And I saw thrones, and they sat upon them, and judgement was given unto them: and I saw the souls of them that were beheaded for the witness of Jesus, and for the word of God, and which had not worshiped the beast, neither his image, neither had received his mark, upon their foreheads, or in their hands; and they lived

> and reigned with Christ a thousand years. But the rest of the dead lived not again until the thousand years were finished. This is the first resurrection. Blessed and holy is he that hath part in the first resurrection: on such the second death hath no power, but they shall be priests of God and of Christ, and shall reign with him a thousand years. (Rev. 20:4–6)

> And I saw the dead, small and great, stand before God; and the books were opened: and another book was opened, which is the book of life: and the dead were judged out of those things which were written in the books, according to their works. And the sea gave up the dead which were in it; and death and hell delivered up the dead which were in them: and they were judged every man according to their works. And death and hell were cast into the lake of fire. This is the second death. And whosoever was not found written in the book of life was cast into the lake of fire. (Rev. 20:12–15)

The resurrection of the just and the unjust will be separated by one thousand years. This one-thousand-year period of time is the kingdom that will feature Jesus the Christ as king. This is the kingdom that the Jewish nation of Israel have been waiting for since their beginning in Israel.

We call the resurrection of the just the rapture, the calling out of those that believe that Jesus is the son of God and that he died to pay the price of redemption, was buried, took our sin to hell, and resurrected to new life in a glorified body to give us eternal life in him.

The rapture is exclusively for the church, the body of Christ. This was revealed to us by Paul.

> For as the body is one, and has many members, and all the members of that one body, being many, are one body: so also is Christ. Now ye are the body of Christ, And members in particular. (1 Cor. 12:12)

> And hath put all things under his feet, and gave him to be the head of all things to the church, Which is his body, the fullness of him that filleth all in all. (Eph. 1:22–23)

> And he is the head of the body, the church: who is the beginning, the firstborn from the dead; that in all things he might have the preeminence. (Col. 1:18)

Jesus explains the parable of the tares and the wheat to his disciples in Matthew 13:37–43 (paraphrased): He that soweth the good seed is the Son of man [Jesus], the field is the world, and the good seed is the children of the kingdom here on earth. The tares are the children of the wicked one [Satan]. Jesus will send his angels to gather out of his kingdom all things that offend and do iniquity and shall cast them into the lake of fire. This will happen at the end of the kingdom age.

> And I say unto you, That many shall come from the east and west, and shall sit down with

> Abraham, and Isaac, and Jacob, in the kingdom of heaven. But the children of the kingdom shall be cast out into outer darkness: there shall be weeping and gnashing of teeth. (Matt. 8:11–12)

Because God will not allow anything into his kingdom that is evil, offensive, or defiling, it is evident that the above scriptures are referring to the end of the kingdom age. This is before the eternal kingdom that will be explained later. So what happened during the kingdom age?

During the seven-year tribulation period, because of the 144,000 Jewish witnesses, many will be saved. Some of these will escape execution and will go into the kingdom, and during that one thousand years, they will not die, and they will have many children that will not die, and so on, producing a population explosion. At this time Satan is in a bottomless pit, chained up and sealed in (Rev. 20:1–3). But at the end of the one thousand years, he will be loosed for a little season.

Satan will gather an army, as many as the sands of the sea, to do battle (Rev. 20:7–9).

Where did all these people come from that followed Satan? These are the children of the kingdom in Matthew 8:12. "But the children of the kingdom shall be cast out into outer darkness: there shall be weeping and gnashing of teeth." How many there are we do not know, but the angels will separate them.

The body of Christ (the church), will be present in the kingdom but will not be subject to the wrath of God during the seven years of the tribulation. The church, also known as the body of Christ, will be in heaven, receiving crowns and other rewards that have been stored up for us. And, of course, we will be attending the wedding feast.

> But God commandeth his love for us, in that, while we were yet sinners Christ died for us, Much more then, being now justified by his blood, we shall be saved from wrath through him. (Rom. 5:8–9)

The wrath of God is poured out upon the earth during the seven years of tribulation that precedes the one-thousand-year kingdom. This is the seventieth week of Daniel, also known as the time of Jacob's trouble.

Since the body of Christ is saved from the wrath of God, we will be resurrected before the tribulation begins. The body of Christ is inferred in Revelation 4:1, where it says "come up hither." The church is not mentioned again until Christ returns in chapter 19.

Who Will Not Be Able to Enter the Kingdom?

> For I say unto you, That except your righteousness exceed the righteousness of the Scribes and the Pharisees, ye shall in no case enter into the kingdom of heaven. (Matt. 5:20)

> Not everyone that saith unto me, Lord, Lord, shall enter into the kingdom of heaven; but he

that doeth the will of my Father which is in heaven. (Matt. 7:21)

And said, Verily I say unto you, Except ye be converted, and become as little children, ye shall not enter into the kingdom of heaven. (Matt. 18:3)

Jesus answered and said unto him, Verily, verily, I say unto thee, Except a man be born again he cannot see the kingdom of God. (John 3;3)

Jesus answered, Verily, verily, I say unto thee, Except a man be born of water and of the Spirit, he cannot enter into the kingdom of God. (John 3:5)

Know ye not that the unrighteous shall not inherit the kingdom of God? Be not deceived: neither fornicators, nor idolaters, nor adulterers, nor effeminate, nor abusers of themselves with mankind, Nor thieves, nor covetous, nor drunkards, nor revilers, nor extortioners, shall inherit the kingdom of God. (1 Cor. 6:9–10)

14

Timelines

God's Plan for Mankind
Timeline A

The prophets did not see the cross. It had not yet been devised. I show the cross here as a representation of where Daniel 9:26 said that the Messiah will be cut off. Most all of chapter 53 of Isaiah speaks of the Messiah's suffering.

Isaiah saw the suffering Messiah and that he would be mistreated and be cut off. Other prophets saw the king Messiah that would rule for one thousand years. For the most part, the Jews are still waiting for the Messiah to come as king. They do not accept that Jesus was also the suffering Messiah. They should have known. Some in the priesthood searched the scriptures diligently as to what the prophets saw. Apparently, they were blinded to what Daniel had said. That seventy weeks of years were determined upon the people of Israel. The time that they were permitted to go back to Jerusalem to rebuild the walls of the city until the Messiah would be cut off would be seven and sixty-two weeks. The seventy weeks of Daniel are seventy weeks of years or four hundred and ninety years, The Messiah was cut off after sixty-nine weeks or four hundred and eighty-three years. This leaves seven years of prophesy left unfulfilled. This seven years is known as the tribulation that is described in the book of Revelation.

Now this is important. The prophets did not see the church age because it had been kept secret in God. (In the gospels, Jesus did not reveal this secret. Everything that he had done was for the benefit of the Jews that were under the law of Moses.) Israel knows of the time of Jacob's trouble, known as the tribulation. They know that it is out there somewhere and after they go through this time, the Messiah would return to be their king in the kingdom of God.

GOD'S PLAN FOR MAN

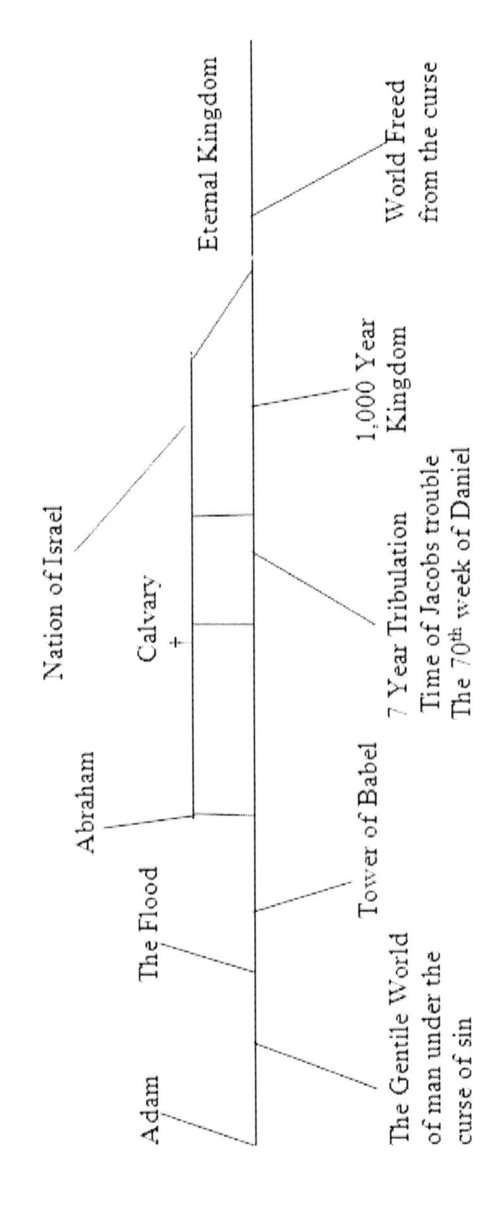
Adam
The Flood
Abraham
Nation of Israel
Calvary
Eternal Kingdom
The Gentile World
of man under the
curse of sin
Tower of Babel
7 Year Tribulation
Time of Jacobs trouble
The 70th week of Daniel
1,000 Year
Kingdom
World Freed
from the curse
Timeline A

Timeline B

Timeline B is the same as timeline A, but the church age is in between the cross and the tribulation. The church has lasted now for almost two thousand years, and it will end when Jesus returns to usher the saved into heaven. We call this the rapture; we just don't know how much longer that might be before he comes.

The church age was a mystery that God revealed to Paul. A mystery in scripture is a secret kept by God until he reveals it at a time of his choosing.

Jesus came into Jerusalem on what we call Palm Sunday as a king riding on a donkey. But he was rejected and crucified. Had they received him as king, there would be no need for timeline B. This was a valid offer. Just as was the time that Israel was at the gate to the Promised Land back in Genesis. God was going to drive out the inhabitants with hornets so that they could enter the land without war, and they would not believe him. So they sent in spies to see what they were up against. And because they didn't believe God, God sent them into the wilderness for forty years. They could have had it all, but they rejected his offer. Again, it was a valid offer. God knew the outcome before he made the offer, yet he did give them a chance.

God's plan for the Jews has not changed. His plans have been put on hold so that God could call out a people for himself: the church. After the church has been raptured out, God's plan for the Jews will continue, beginning with the tribulation, the time of Jacob's trouble.

Church added but God's plan for Israel is unchanged:

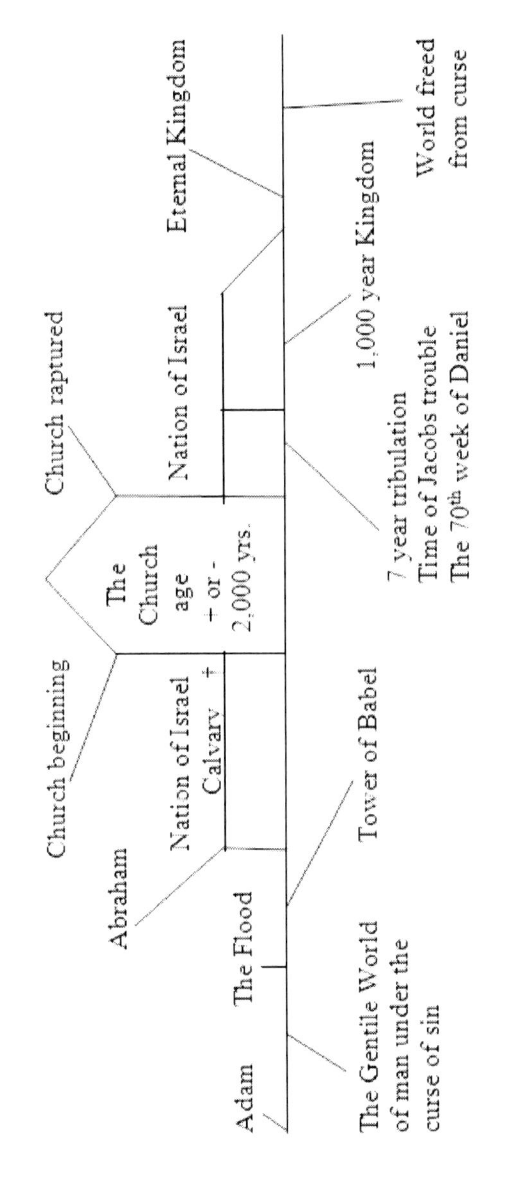
Church added but
God's plan for Israel
Is unchanged
Church beginning
Church raptured
Abraham
Nation of Israel
Calvary
The
Church
age
+ or -
2,000 yrs.
Nation of Israel
Eternal Kingdom
Adam
The Flood
Tower of Babel
1,000 year Kingdom
World freed
from curse
The Gentile World
of man under the
curse of sin
7 year tribulation
Time of Jacobs trouble
The 70th week of Daniel

Timeline B

Timeline C

What happens after the rapture of the church? Israel will sign a peace treaty with the Antichrist for seven years, but they won't know that it is the Antichrist. This starts the tribulation period that will last for seven years.

Israel will rebuild the temple and again institute temple worship under the law of Moses. They will think that this man is the Messiah as he rules the world in peace. At the midpoint of the seven years, the Antichrist will break the peace treaty and he will defile the temple, possibly by offering a pig as a sacrifice. The last three and a half years will be full of God's wrath. They will also suffer the wrath of Satan; he knows that his time is short. The whole human race will go into this seven-year period except for those that have been raptured. Because of the 144,000 witnesses, many will be saved, and many of those will be killed.

Only those that are written in the Lamb's Book of Life will enter the kingdom of God. This is the church that was raptured and those that are still alive at the end of the seven years. Those that are still alive still have flesh and blood. Flesh and blood cannot enter the kingdom of God. In Luke 24:39 Jesus does not say flesh and blood, but he said flesh and bone. I might point out here that sin is in the blood, and that is why blood will not be in the final kingdom. Also that is why we will have a new body in the rapture. Satan is now cast into the bottomless pit, he will be chained up until the end of the one-thousand-year kingdom, and then he shall be loosed for a little season.

During this time no one will die, and these flesh-and-blood people will have children, and their children will have children, and on and on for one thousand years, and none will die. Now that is a lot of generations of people, resulting in a great population explosion. These billions of people have had no concept of evil. Remember, Satan is bound in the bottomless pit.

At the end of the one thousand years, Satan will be released for a little season. These billions of people (who have never been given the opportunity to choose between good and evil) will be confronted with Satan. Not the Satan with a pitchfork, but he will be as an angel of light. And just as he deceived Eve in the garden of eden, many will follow him.

He (Satan) gathers a large army to go against the king (Jesus). Satan is defeated, and he is thrown into the lake of fire where the beast and the false prophet are. Here there is an unknown period of time at the end of the one-thousand-year reign of Christ. All of the people on earth will be evacuated up to heaven, the lost will be judged according to the books in heaven, and then they will be cast into the Lake of Fire. This is known as the Great White Throne judgement.

During this time the earth is being tried by fire. A new heaven and a new earth are now ready for the final kingdom of God.

As I see it there are three kingdoms of God. There is the one that now exists in heaven, one coming soon that will last one thousand years, and the third is the kingdom in eternity. As God is three personalities in one, each having a different function; the kingdom is also three in one, each a different function in different time periods. In the first and third kingdoms there is no blood. Sin is in the blood.

> Now this I say, brethren, that flesh and blood cannot inherit the kingdom of God; neither doth corruption inherit incorruption. (1 Cor. 15:50)

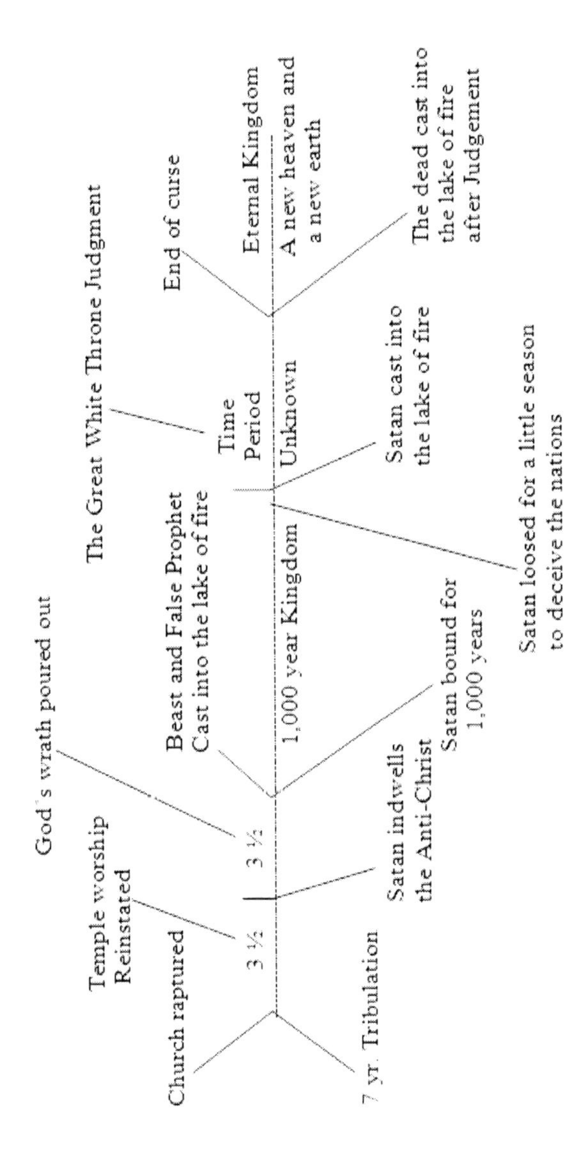
After the rapture of the Church
Church raptured
7 yr. Tribulation
Temple worship
Reinstated
3 ½
3 ½
Satan indwells
the Anti-Christ
God's wrath poured out
Beast and False Prophet
Cast into the lake of fire
1,000 year Kingdom
Satan bound for
1,000 years
The Great White Throne Judgment
Time
Period
Unknown
Satan cast into
the lake of fire
Satan loosed for a little season
to deceive the nations
End of curse
Eternal Kingdom
A new heaven and
a new earth
The dead cast into
the lake of fire
after Judgement

Timeline C

15

Conclusion and What's Next?

Conclusion

I could have included many more subjects from the Bible in this short book. My goal herein was to get you interested in reading your Bible and learning, with the help of the Holy Spirit, what God has revealed to us. Also to lead you, the reader, to a saving knowledge of our Lord and Savior, Jesus Christ. Now one more analogy, then I will lead you down the Roman's road.

In Leviticus 23 God gives instructions to Moses about the harvest. There are the firstfruits, the main harvest, and the gleanings. In the firstfruits, some of the grain ripens first throughout the field. They were to gather these ripe sheaves and bundle them together and make a sheaf offering to the Lord. Then, when the field was fully ripe, they were to harvest the main crop, leaving the corners as well as any that fell to the ground during the harvest. This leftover crop of grain was to be left for the poor and needy.

The firstfruits represents Christ after his resurrection, along with those souls that were in paradise. The main harvest is the rapture of the church [the body of Christ]. And the gleanings are those souls under the altar of God in the book of Revelation, called the tribulation saints.

You were not in the resurrection of the firstfruits. The question then is, Are you going to be in the main harvest, called the rapture of the church? Or are you going to take a chance on being in the gleanings? If so, you can expect to be beheaded in order to show your allegiance to God and not to the beast in Revelation, Satan. I don't like the idea of being in this latter group, and I don't think that you do either. Why take the risk?

The other day, my granddaughter Ashlynne and I were having a conversation. During this conversation I made the comment that I was perfect in Christ. And she said to me that no one was perfect. Of course she is right. Only Christ is perfect. She did not understand the part about being perfect in Christ. God makes us perfect when we receive Him as our Lord and Savior. So that you understand your position with God, I will now take you down the Roman's road.

The Roman's road is a number of scriptures taken from the book of Romans written by Paul.

> As it is written, There is none righteous, no, not one (Rom 3:10).

> For all have sinned, and come short of the glory of God (Rom. 3:23).

> For the wages of sin is death; but the gift of God is eternal life through Jesus Christ our Lord (Rom. 6:23).
>
> But God commandeth his love toward us, in that, while we were yet sinners, Christ died for us (Rom. 5:8).
>
> That if thou shalt confess with thy mouth the Lord Jesus Christ, and shalt believe in thine heart that God hath raised him from the dead, thou shalt be saved (Rom. 10:9).

No one is righteous; every one of us have sinned, every one falls short of God's glory. We deserve to die a spiritual death because we are sinners. Even though we are sinners, God sent his son, Jesus, to die in our place to pay that penalty of death that we earned. And by our receiving this payment for our sin, God has taken us as his children. Our salvation is by our faith in what Christ has done for us; it is all about him.

I am sure that I will shock some of you here in my next statement. No one will ever go to hell because of their sin. That, of course, includes murders, rapist, thieves, and any other degenerate that you can think of. Jesus paid our sin debt in full. We don't have to ask Jesus to forgive us of our sin because he has already done so. To ask him to do it again implies that he did not do it right the first time. When you confess your sin to Jesus, just thank him for his forgiveness.

People go to hell because they have not accepted the payment that God provided for them. Since they rejected God, they chose to go to hell not for their sin, but because of rejection. I urge you to accept God's plan for your salvation now. Pray this prayer, and receive Jesus into your heart right now:

> God, I confess that I am a sinner, and I do not deserve your forgiveness. I accept Jesus as my personal savior, and I ask you Jesus to come into my heart right now and save me.
>
> Thank you for forgiving me and saving me. Amen.

What's Next?

Hopefully you have read my book on the Bible. So what happens to me if Christ comes again and raptures the believers to spend eternity with him and I am still here? What next? What do I have to look forward to? Is there any hope for me, or am I eternally lost? I thought that I was a child of God! I went to church every week, paid my tithes, said my prayers, and fed hungry people at the soup kitchen. I was kind and caring towards other people. I don't understand why God would do this to me!

Throughout the Bible God has said that a remnant shall be saved. That was true for Israel, and that is also true for all others, known as Gentiles. Here in America about 25–30% of us are affiliated with a church of one denomination or another. (We call ourselves Christians.) Out of this one hundred million, only a remnant will be saved. I am being generous here in saying that 10% of these are truly born again.

> Because strait is the gate and narrow is the way, which leadeth unto life, and few there be that find it. (Matt. 7:14)

> Not everyone that saith unto me, Lord, Lord, shall enter into the kingdom of heaven; but he that doeth the will of my Father which is in heaven. Many will say to me in that day, Lord, Lord, have we not prophesied in your name? and in thy name have cast out devils? and in thy name done many wonderful works? And then will I profess unto them, I never knew you: depart from me, ye that work iniquity. (Matt. 7:21–23)

It will be devastating to millions of people that have been left behind to hear these words: "I never knew you."

Houston, we have a problem! Now you may be thinking of Apollo 13, the ill-fated space trip to the moon, and this is true. Okay, in fact, I have a problem. All of a sudden my wife is gone. Where did she go? Did she leave me without leaving me a note? Everything seemed to be okay last night when we went to bed. I can't believe this is happening to me. Okay, why am I being so paranoid? She probably just got up early to go get some groceries before it got to crowded. But why are her PJs still here in bed beside me where she should be? Oh, well, I will just get a cup of coffee and watch GMA till she gets back.

What's that? Millions of people around the world are mysteriously missing as the news scrolls by at the bottom of the screen. Could this be the rapture as some Christians believe?

Wow, if this is the rapture, then I missed it. But why? We went to church together, took our kids every Sunday—even when we were on vacation. We believed the same things. I knew that Jesus died for all of our sins. Why did God take her and leave me behind? He knew God in his head. She knew God in her heart.

Believing in God is one thing, and believing God is another. People around the world believe in God. Their god may be different than the God that you believe in. Yes, most people believe there is a god. The Greeks, the Romans, and many other nationalities have several gods. The sun god, mother earth, the fertility god, Allah—the list goes on and on. But for my point here, let's talk about the one true God of this universe: the Christian's God, the creator and sustainer of all life. This is the God that you and I believe in.

Now believing in God is universal in the Christian church, but believing God is an individual act of obedience. All through the years of your life in your learning about God is called head knowledge (universal, we understand who God is). Believing God is to take him at his word on a personal basis—this is heart knowledge. The man's wife had a personal relationship with God in the person of his son, Jesus.

The man himself knew who God was but did not have a personal relationship with him.

So you may be a person that has spent years of your life in church, in Sunday school, reading the Bible, etc. However, you have been left behind—"Now what can I expect to happen to me?"

I am glad you asked. There is now coming a period of time called the tribulation that will last for seven years. This is a period of time that was set apart for the Jewish nonbelievers. Unfortunately, you that are left behind will also go through this devastating period of time. At the end of this, the world will transition into another fixed period of time called the millennial reign of Christ (*millennial* meaning one thousand years). After this will be the judgment seat of Christ, and all that are judged will be cast into the lake of fire, which will be far worse than hell itself (Rev. 6:9–11). Fortunately, God is merciful, and many during this time will be saved. However, many will suffer death by beheading for not accepting the mark of the beast or Antichrist (Rev. 13:17, 20:4). If you do not bow down and worship this person, you will be beheaded. You cannot buy or sell anything unless you have his mark in your forehead or hand (most likely a computer chip).

If you receive this mark so that you can buy groceries, gas, and pay your bills, you will be showing your allegiance to this man that is called Antichrist, and you cannot be saved.

So if you find yourself in this position, do not receive this mark or worship this man. You may starve to death or have to go into hiding. Your next-door neighbor or your friends will turn you in to receive a reward from the Antichrist. If so, you will be given another chance to receive the mark, and if you refuse, you will be beheaded.

You will face a decision that you should have made before the rapture of the church—that being to receive Jesus Christ as your personal savior. You would have become a child of God, been afforded his divine protection, and received rewards and eternal life. You would be in heaven now instead of this awful choice that has come before you.

Since you did not receive Christ, you are given the opportunity to receive him now and have your head cut off. Or refuse him and live to be later thrown into the lake of fire. Not a good position to be in, but losing your life now by beheading is better than the lake of fire for eternity. Fifty percent of the people on earth will die during this seven-year period. It will be a horrific seven years to live through with all the devastation. I hope you make it.

Do not receive the mark of the beast nor worship him in any way.

God be with you. Amen.

(Read again the conclusion of my book.)

CPSIA information can be obtained at www.ICGtesting.com
Printed in the USA
LVOW11s0814070816

499259LV00004B/6/P

9 781682 549490